Life On Purpose

Reflections

Teresa Moore

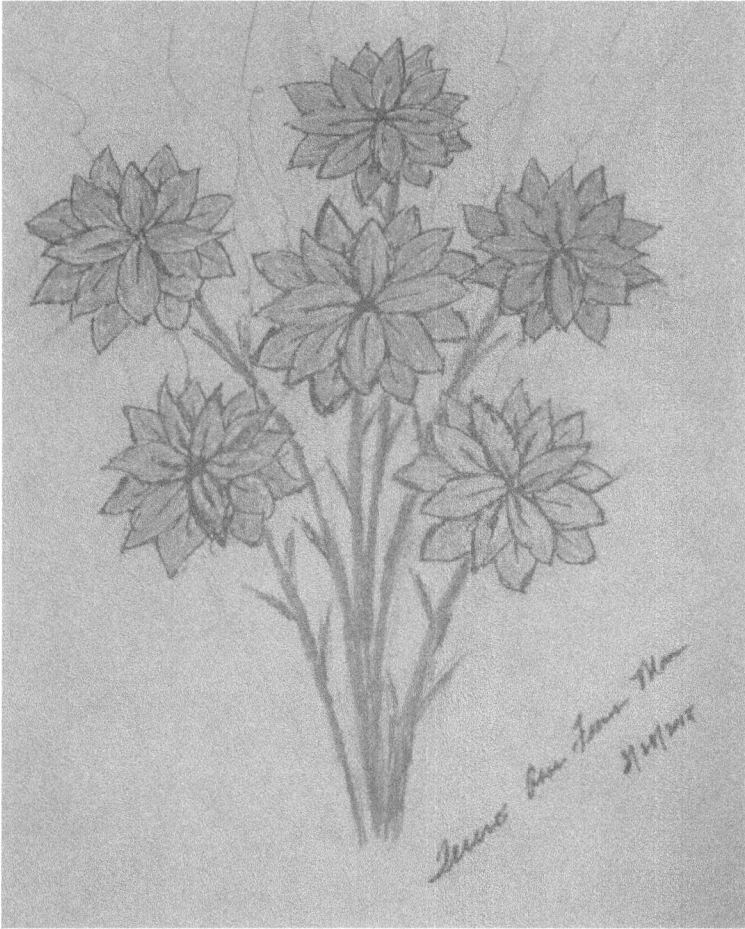

DEDICATION

First and foremost, I dedicate this book to God, omnipotent, omniscient, omnipresent, omnibenevolent, Great Organizing Deity, of all that exists. Without God, my life would lack meaning and purpose. I love you.

Second, I dedicate this book to my family who love me no matter what. I love you.

Lastly, I dedicate this book to all who open their hearts, minds, and spirits to this magnificent thing called life, who spend their lives looking for the lessons and joy even when they may appear hidden.

CONTENTS

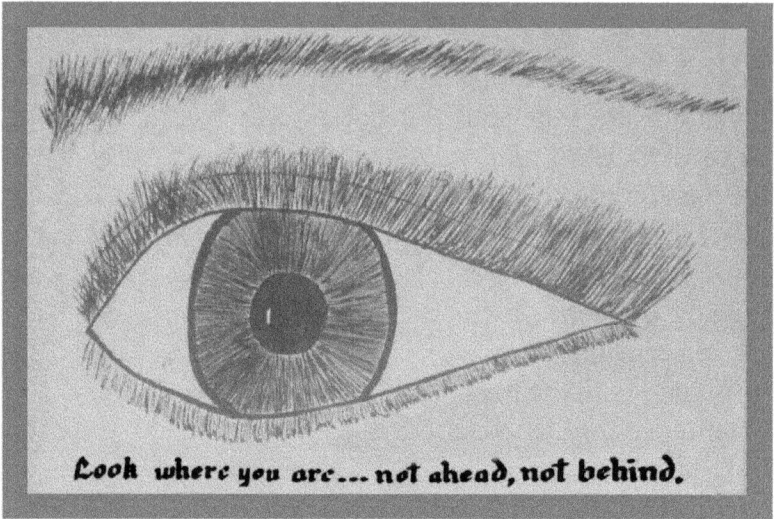

Look where you are ... not ahead, not behind.

ABOUT THE COVER ART

I could write an entire book about the symbolism represented in this one drawing. Briefly, multiple physical symbols are present including the ancient symbol of the vesica pisces represented by the almond shape of the eye and the implied lens of the eye, the circles seen in both the iris and pupil, and the rainbow forming the iris.

Through the ages, the eye has been thought of as the window into the soul. I used the eye to represent this as well as "vision," and the ability to "see." The sacred geometry of the ancient symbol, the vesica pisces (formed by the intersection of two circles with the same radius) is fascinating; here it represents the connection between the Divine and the physical. The circles represent unity, wholeness, and all that is. As so eloquently put by Hermes Trismegistus, "God is a circle whose centre is everywhere and whose circumference is nowhere." A circular rainbow forms the iris, which physically controls how much light is allowed to enter our eyes, and metaphorically begs us to consider how much light we are willing to see and let enter our lives. The use of the rainbow again echoes the connection of the earthly plane with the heavenly plane and the hope promised by the appearance of the rainbow after the great flood.

The statement underneath the eye, is to remind us to be present to the eternal now.

Simply, this art is about vision, acceptance and allowing, wholeness, the separation and unification of the sacred and the profane that can only be experienced when we open our souls to all that is, on all levels, planes, and dimensions, while concurrently existing in the eternal now.

ACKNOWLEDGMENTS

First, I would like to thank God for allowing me to live in this physical body, on this planet, at this time. It's a great time to be on spaceship Earth.

My parents have loved me as long as I have existed, and their love has infused every bit of my being. They have been supportive even when we have had differing opinions. To them, I say eternally, "Thank you."

Eugene, thank you for all of the things that you have done that have allowed me to write, to paint, to attend sweat lodges, and to continuously evolve into me. Though we look at life differently, you have always given me the space to be me. That is priceless. We also created three amazing children together. Thank you.

To my children, Jeremy, Cameron, and Alexa, you have been such a blessing and have taught me so much about life and loving. Thank you for putting up with me, especially when I seemed to ignore you in order to write.

Jackie, my loving sister, thank you for being you. Without you, I would not be me.

My friends, though we are not blood related, we are family. Because of space limitations, I can only mention a few who have traveled this journey with me. Rana, you know all of me and love me anyway, no matter what. Thank you! To my sweat lodge family, especially Joan and Angie, thank you for letting me be part of something that fills my soul and keeps me connected to Spirit. BB, you know who you are, and what you mean to me. Heather, thanks for Saturday morning swims. Kat, thanks for being you and for offering so much of you to the world. Sandie, I could not have done this without your help as my house would have been uninhabitable and my heart would not be as warm. To my many other friends, thank you for enriching my journey.

Lastly, I would like to thank JoAnne and John for introducing me to Ruth and Debbie. Because of them and their vision of Turning Point Healing Retreat Center, and of TurningPointHealing.org, I have faced insecurities and overcome procrastination, compiling some of my newspaper articles into this book that you now hold in your hands. Enough said.

PREFACE

Just like yin and yang, life balances itself, containing the light within the dark and the dark within the light. We judge things as good or bad based on our personal perspectives, when in reality, they simply exist. We may become so overwhelmed with the minutia or unimportant things that we forget to pay attention to the things that really are important. If we are willing to dig into all that is, without labeling it, we may find that piece of wisdom that is more precious than jewels or gold. We may awaken to the joy intermingled with the tears. This is life on purpose.

Though I have been passionate about reading and writing since childhood, I did not believe that I could write well or that anyone would want to read what I had to say. After all, many of my graded English papers came back to me looking as though they had lined a battlefield peppered with casualties, bloody red with corrections. Despite this, my last semester in college I took a paper-heavy class, "The Complete Works of Shakespeare," in which we read all of his plays and most of his major sonnets in one semester. While concurrently interviewing for medical school and taking multiple graduate level courses in genetics, I took the Shakespeare class pass/fail because I did not want a poor grade in an elective class. Halfway through the semester, the seasoned professor called me to her office to express her disapproval of my choice to take the class pass/fail instead of for a grade. I explained my reasoning, and she complemented my writing highly, noting that it made her "sick to simply pass" me. Then, she asked if I had ever considered being a writer. Being young and dumb, I believed that her comments were spoken out of politeness. Only years later did I come to realize that she had been sincere.

When she called me to her office, I had not been ready to hear, nor to believe, what she said because of my insecurities. Also, if I had contemplated her words, they would have disrupted my anticipated journey along the life path stretching out in front of me.

So I carefully packed her comments away into my memory, undisturbed until I woke one night with a poem inside of me. Jumping out of bed, running to my computer, I typed furiously to capture it at 3:30 A.M. Once complete, I submitted it to a publisher. Eventually, I figured out that I had submitted it to a vanity press. That didn't matter to my heart or soul as I got the letter from them telling me that they were going to publish it. I burst into tears of joy, my heart opened, and I felt the previously elusive emotions that I had expected to feel when I graduated college and medical school. Another path lay at my feet. Did I have the courage to walk down it?

About this time, I hired a life coach, Kathleen Brehony, Ph.D., who is also a writer, and she helped me immensely. Encouraged by Kathleen, I stepped over fear, took a deep breath, prepared for rejection, and approached Averett Jones, editor of my local paper, the Southside Messenger, about writing a philosophical column. Much to my happiness, surprise, and joy, he said yes. I spent the next five years putting my thoughts onto paper and into my column, "Life on Purpose." Many of these articles were picked up by the Charlottesville paper, ECHO, as well.

Over time, life got busy, and eventually I stopped writing consistently due to exhaustion from working excessive hours in a medical practice. In doing so, I misplaced a part of me. Years later, during one of my own turning points, synchronicity brought the founders of Turning Point Healing Retreat Center into my life. Always desiring to be of service, I gifted some of these articles to be published in book format to help them with fundraising, and in the process of reviewing these thoughts I had written years ago, I have found me and my strength once again.

I hope these pages will help you just the same. I hope they make you smile, cry, feel, and reflect. I have no answers for you, only questions and thoughts to help you clarify your own. I hope that you find your own spark of divinity even if it is hidden deep within. I know that it is there, and deep down, so do you.

Section One: Lessons From Kids

BLOSSOMING

Before a flower becomes a flower, it is a seed, full of potential. Plant the seed in soil, water it, expose it to light, and it will reveal its beauty over time. Flowers grow into the flowers that they are destined to become. A carnation becomes a carnation. A rose becomes a rose. The seeds simply germinate into the perfection that is. Over time, roots form, and the seedling bursts forth from the earth as if to say, "World, here I come." The stem grows towards the light and eventually the flower bursts forth, facing that light directly. If bugs eat the plant's leaves or if an animal partly destroys the plant, either the plant lives or it doesn't. If the plant lives, than that plant grows as best it can from what is left after the trauma. Many times the plant is even stronger after the trauma. The flowers bloom in their own time, singularly beautiful, together breathtaking.

Just like a flower, each of us starts out as a seed of our future selves containing the potentiality to grow into ourselves. We start out similarly to the flower, needing food like the seed needs soil, milk as an infant and water thereafter, and a source of light/love to provide for us until we can sustain ourselves. We each experience the harshness of life as do the flowers, albeit in different ways. When we are able to survive these traumas, we grow often stronger than we were prior to the trauma. As we blossom into our own unique forms, some of us face the world singularly, standing alone; others exist in family units. Collectively we grow into the unique garden that we call humanity.

Warm All Over

A few years ago, while laying in the bed cuddling my daughter, Alexa, I said, "It's cold." Immediately, Alexa proceeded to pull the covers up over me, and then piled all of the pillows on top of me. Happy with her effort, she said, "Are you warm now Mommy?" The chill had left my body, and my heart was overcome with warmness. She had responded to my comment with genuine love and compassion although it was uttered only as a statement about the overall temperature. I wondered if I would have responded so quickly, and with such love, or would I have just adjusted her covers out of obligation and responsibility if she had made the comment. In reality, I could have responded either way depending on the time of the day, my general level of energy, and other things competing for my time. Alexa, at this stage in her life, responded to the moment with total awareness and unconditional love.

What began as me talking out loud, transformed into a beautiful lesson from the universe about paying attention and about need fulfillment. Even though I had not actually been thinking about piling on more covers, Alexa heard my musing, realized that she could fulfill it, and she did just that on multiple levels. Physically, I was toasty warm. Mentally, emotionally, and spiritually, my heart had warmed even more.

Often what we say we want in life has to do with the physical world. We want more money, time, or stuff. We want the weather to be warmer or colder. We wish for satisfying work. We want a comfort and ambience. Though these things are important in some respects, usually, our soul's desire has little to do with the physical world. Often we get our physical desires fulfilled and yet remain emotionally and spiritually empty. No amount of physical gratification can fill that void; only genuine connection with our true essence and with the universal creative force can. After these connections have been made we have the opportunity to share this with others as Alexa shared with me that night when she covered me up with the blankets.

In some ways, it is easier to desire things on the physical level because we feel as though we have some control over these things. If we work harder and make the right connections, we think that we can obtain these things. When our desires are to be loved, respected, accepted, and appreciated for who we truly are, we feel emotionally vulnerable as we look for these things outside of ourselves. Paradoxically, these desires can never be filled externally. It is only when we find these things internally on a spiritual level that we can share them with others, and we can never offer or receive more of these things than we have shared with ourselves.

This week, think about what your current emotional and spiritual needs are. If you desire more love from others, reflect on how much love you have for yourself. If you can't muster up love for yourself, how can you receive it or share it with another? If you want acceptance from others, consider whether you have accepted yourself. If you want respect from others, think about whether you have respect for yourself and for others. Then realize that what you want emotionally, is usually what others want as well. It is only when we offer the world our true selves that we will find these things and be able to share them. As you go through your days, pay attention to other's needs for these same things. As you unconditionally give of yourself to others, you will find that even more of it is mirrored back to you.

Scars from Falling Down

Years ago, I played hide and seek with my children. During one of my turns as "It," I spotted one of them trying to sneak out of his hiding place, and I jolted towards him. Exhilaration coursed through my veins as I quickly ran towards him. Suddenly, I flew through the air and landed face down in the gravel after tripping on a piece of wood that "Not me" had left lying in the gravel. As my kids ran over to ensure that I was okay, after telling me that they were safe because they had already touched base, all I could do was tell them to let me lie there for a while as I assessed my injuries. After catching my breath, (the fall had knocked the wind out of me) I sat up slowly. Surprisingly, I had gotten only a bruised left knee and right thigh along with a few scratches on my hands and legs. As I brushed the dirt off, I got up only slightly worse for the wear, smiling all the while.

I was smiling because I was having so much fun playing with them. Sometimes, I played games with them while thinking about all the other things that I need to do. This game was different and much more fun. I was fully present, playing with intent to catch them, running instead of walking. (Quite often in the past, after finding them, I would slowly and carefully walk towards them while going through my mental to do list.) This time, even though my body hurled through the air, crash landing into the gravel, still sore from the adventure, I am so thankful for the experience. I still haven't forgotten the adrenaline pumping through me while running, nor the smell of the gravel, nor the concerned faces up above me as I lay there. Every bit of that total experience is cemented into my memory with precise detail.

Why is it that that memory is so vivid and delightful even though the end result seems to be pain and injury? I believe that the outcome of the event had very little to do with it. Instead, it is because I was fully present to the whole experience, from counting to thirty, with my eyes closed and ears perked, to the sudden sting as my bare skin collided with the gravel, that it has engraved itself into me. Even when it hurt to move my neck because of the impact, I couldn't stop smiling about it.

As I reflected on this experience, I fondly remembered how scars help us to tell our life stories. My children will ask about one of my scars, and a story of how I got it emerges. Though these scars are physical, all scars, mental, emotional, physical, and spiritual, shape our lives. These scars may be associated with pain or joy. Once the scar is present, we will never be exactly as we were before it occurred, and we can choose how to experience the scar. It is a part of our story, and we can use it as a springboard to growth or as an explanation of our misery. What happened to cause the scar cannot change, only how we choose to re-experience and use it can.

For the next week, consider how your life would change if you created new and more uplifting associations for the scars in your life? I don't mean that it was not painful, or that you should deny or distort what happened to cause it, only that you may look for whatever good came out of the situation. By doing so, you may find joy where you expected to find pain and beauty where you had previously seen blemishes.

Piercing Through Fear

For several years my daughter, Alexa, had politely declined getting her ears pierced saying that she was not ready. Then one Saturday, she decided that she was ready. Not a daylight hour passed without her asking me, "Mommy, when can I get my ears pierced? Can we go now?" until the day that she got them pierced. As I saw the mixture of fear and elation in her eyes as her ears were marked with purple dots, I traveled back in time to the day that my mom took me to get my ears pierced. That feeling of wanting something so badly and still being afraid of the process that was required to get it is still palpable today. Click. One was done. It hurt a little. Click, it was over. Alexa smiled, celebrating her pierced ears as she looked from ear to ear in the mirror.

As I sat with her holding her little hands, I saw her face her fear that day. Until then she had been unready to do it. Once she was ready, there was no stopping her. Before she was ready, no amount of pleading, persuading, or begging would convince her that she could face her fear of getting her ears pierced. Only her own knowing and her own desire was enough to convince her to push forward past her fears into the land of her dreams. Once she mastered her fear, she was ready to celebrate her conquest with the world and anyone who wanted to share in her joy.

Alexa spent years too afraid to get her ears pierced, and about three minutes actually sitting in the hot seat getting them pierced. Then, she spent weeks celebrating her pierced ears, and the elation of overcoming the fear. Just as she spent time in each of three stages, most of our lives are spent in one of these three stages. There is the time spent anticipating facing the fear. Then there is the time spent facing the fear. Lastly, there is the time spent celebrating the conquest of the fear.

The time spent facing the fear is usually not the lengthiest though it is the most dreaded; thus, the time spent anticipating the fear may last from seconds to years depending on the urgency of the situation even when the time that it would require to face the fear is measurable in seconds. Once we have faced our fears, many of us do not take the time to honor our courage and bravery. Unfortunately, when we forget to celebrate the conquest of our fears, it seems as though our entire life is spent in the proverbial lions' den. We spend precious time dreading what facing our fear will require, then survive it just as another fear provoking situation pops up. Living in fear uses so much vital time and energy that it can hinder our soul's growth for years or even lifetimes. Celebration reminds us why we choose to face our fears and gives us a reason to push through them...the hope that we can make our lives, our planet, and our universe even better.

Though we believe that most of our fears are more significant than those of a child getting her ears pierced, they really aren't that much different. In fact, some children have faced more fears in a few years than other adults are able to face in a lifetime. It is the courage that we gain by facing our fears that spurs us on to do even more difficult things. As long as we avoid doing what we fear, the fear controls us and our lives. The more we celebrate the conquest of our fears, the more we create and enjoy our own lives.

For the next week, consider your own fears. How would your life change if you faced your own fears? Are you willing to face the discomfort of facing them head on? Are the fears there to protect you from harm or to hinder your growth? Honor them if they provide needed safety and pierce through them if they are blocking your soul's evolution.

These Shoes Make Me Look Beautiful

When my daughter Alexa was about three, we went out shopping for a new pair of shoes as she was quickly outgrowing all that she had. After picking out a new pair of sneakers and sandals, she brought another pair to me and said, "Mommy, I need these." At that time, she was wearing a size seven or eight shoe. The shoes she brought me were size thirteen. They were wedged sandals with a band of peach, melon, and white sequins that stretched across the forefoot. After twenty to thirty minutes of searching for these shoes in an appropriate size, I came to the conclusion that this was the only pair of shoes like that in the store. I explained that these shoes would not fit her, and asked if she wanted another somewhat glitzy pair that was available in her size. She said, "No. I want this pair. They make me look beautiful."

In vain, I explained that she is beautiful in any shoes. Though she expressed understanding that she is beautiful, she continued to explain that those shoes made her look beautiful. At the time, I did not quite understand what she meant, and yet she was determined to get those shoes. She even offered to put back the other two pairs of shoes that actually fit her just so that she could have the sequined pair. After seeing how much those shoes meant to her, I decided that she could have that pair also though I expected them to sit in her closet for a few years until she could fit into them. She had a different idea.

She wore those shoes almost everywhere and with anything. Soon after she got them, I saw her running across the gravel driveway. I yelled, "Stop running in those shoes. I'm afraid that you'll fall down and get hurt." She hollered back, "It's okay Mommy. I can run in these shoes without getting hurt." With clenched teeth, I let it go silently praying for her safety while still fearing that I would have to pick her up and clean gravel out of her scraped knees. Much to my surprise, she ran swiftly and without hesitation in those shoes, and she remained scratch-free that day.

As she grew, those shoes traveled many places with her. It mattered little that the soles stuck out three inches beyond her heel. Whenever she wore them, she transformed into even more of a princess. Her eyes sparkled a little extra. She pranced with even more glee than usual. I came to realize what she meant over time. Even though she is beautiful to me all of the time, she feels beautiful in those shoes. It is this feeling of exuberance that the shoes gave her. It is the feeling that she wanted even though she thought that it was the shoes.

Eventually, I saw her put on an old ragged pair of sequined sandals that she had finally grown into. Though they looked anything but beautiful to me, she still adored them and wore them as often as possible. She had long outgrown the other two pairs of shoes that she had gotten on the same day, and though I don't even remember what they looked like, I'll never forget this pair.

It is not what anyone else saw when they looked at those shoes that mattered to her. What mattered is that those shoes made her feel beautiful, and when a person feels beautiful in such an innocent way, it shines through to the world. If I could, I would find her a new pair for her to grow into, and yet those shoes were one of a kind and irreplaceable. Just as I hope that Alexa finds another pair of shoes that make her feel like she looks beautiful, I hope that you find the shoes, pants, shirt, hat, etc. that makes you feel like you really are, beautiful.

For the next week, consider what makes you feel beautiful. What is it about the item that makes you feel beautiful? Would others say that it makes you beautiful? Does their opinion matter?

Playing HORSE

Years ago, I played a game of HORSE with my children. If you are not familiar with this game, it is a basketball game in which successive shooters attempt to replicate the lead shooters shot. If the first player misses his shot, then the second, third, etc. continue to shoot in turn until someone makes a shot. The first person making her shot becomes the lead shooter. One by one, each player attempts the same shot. If the other players miss it, then they individually accrue one letter of the word HORSE. If they make the shot, then play continues with each player shooting the same shot until it is back to the lead shooter. Once the lead shooter misses a shot, then other players continue to shoot until someone makes a shot. Then that person becomes the lead shooter. When you spell HORSE, you are out of the game. The winner is the player that does not spell HORSE.

Now, I am horrible at basketball, and yet I love this game. As a child, I almost always lost this game, and now as adult, occasionally I win. You see, as a child, I played against other children, most of who had much more skill than I did. As an adult playing against my young children, my skills only seemed better as my children had just started playing.

Several things enchant me about this game. Even a long game of HORSE can be played in a short amount of time. It encourages creativity. One of my children likes to shoot the one-handed shots while one of them shoots while bending over backwards. It is fun to see their interaction as we try to mimic each other's shots. Emotions run from despair at missing the easy shot to elation at making the shot that seemed impossible. At times there is wholehearted support of each other that can boil down to an each for his own mentality near the end of the game.

This game is like life in that you take your skills into account as you take calculated risks. Creativity comes into play, as does determination. There are moments of team spirit and then moments when personal desires are front line. In the end, win or lose, fun is the goal. As children, we remember that life is supposed to be fun. Often as adults, we forget that the goal is fun and joy. We get over-focused on winning or achieving in other ways. We forget that we can play together and have fun whether we win or lose.

For the next week, consider how life is like a game of HORSE. As you accomplish personal goals or see others accomplish theirs even when you don't accomplish yours, can and will you cheer for yourself and for them? Can you laugh at the ridiculous and hold onto hope when it seems impossible? Can you see the joy in life and keep a playful attitude even when it seems that you are losing or are out of the game? Can you accept that your skill level is where it is, and that there are those with greater and lesser skills than yourself? Can you accept it when someone with lesser talent or skill and more determination or focus surpasses you? Can you be a good sport when you lose?

When We Fail To See

When I was a child, I had to get eyeglasses. My vision loss had been slow, and I had unknowingly compensated for it in other ways for a long time given the severity of my visual deficit at the time of its initial diagnosis. At twenty feet, I could see what the average person could see from two hundred feet. Only after other people noticed that I was having difficulty seeing, did I notice it. Even then I did not realize how much I had been missing until after I got my glasses. Though I really did not like the idea of having to wear glasses, I was amazed by what I could see with them. On the car ride home from getting my glasses, I remember looking into the sky, and saying, "So that's what birds look like when they fly." I could actually see the individual branches in the trees. The clouds became discreet entities instead of veins of white marbling the blue sky. I could actually see the softball as it came toward me, instead of as it hit me.

As my first child got his first pair of glasses, it reminded me of what I had experienced. I started to wonder what else we miss in life because we really are not able to see what surrounds us. And I am not only talking about what we miss with our physical vision.

We fail to see the effects of pollution in our world, turning a blind eye to noise pollution, air pollution, and land pollution. We miss the suffering all around us as we see the commercials about starving children in other parts of the world. We overlook adults publicly threatening their children, saying, "If you don't stop crying, I'll give you a reason to cry when we get home," just as those parents overlook the child's reason for crying. We may justify our blind sightedness, ambivalence, or obliviousness by telling ourselves that we should not get involved with other people's public lives or that these are not our problems.

We may also overlook much good in the world. Do you see the love in your child's eyes as they give you a hand-picked flower? Or the love that your pet has for you as they get hair or mud on your clothes? Do you see your own prosperity and the kindness that others bestow on you? And if you see it with your eyes, are you seeing it with your heart?

For the next week, pretend that you have been blind to all that is around you, both the positive and the negative. Then imagine that someone gifts you with physical vision and heart vision. For a moment, look around. Pay attention and see with your physical vision first. What do you notice that you have previously overlooked? Then look with your heart. For example, physically you may notice that you have more stuff than you noticed before which initially translates into clutter. As you use your heart vision, you may see abundance. If you see litter on the ground, you can choose to see an opportunity to be a loving caretaker of the land, and pick it up. Over time, practice doing this with more difficult things such as seeing the love in your child's eyes as they bring you handfuls of flowers from the plants that you just finished painstakingly planting. If you hear someone publicly being cruel to a child, you may choose to lovingly intervene. Using heart vision, you may even find a way to see those muddy paw and foot prints as tokens of affection.

It's Possible

One day my son Cameron had done something so sweet that I hugged him and squeezed him and said, "I love you." He looked up at me with those big eyes, smiled and said, "I love you more," to which I replied, "It's not possible." This grin came over his face for a second, which was quickly replaced with a serious look, that means pay attention. He peered deeply into my eyes, took my chin into his hands, and said, "It's possible." Then he ran off playing. Ever since then, each time that I tell Cameron that I love him, his stock reply without batting an eye is "I love you more. It's possible."

Tears of joy welled up in my eyes as he said this. At first, I thought that his words resonated with my soul because of his expression of love; my heart feels like it grows another size each time I hear those words. After hearing these statements several times, I realized that the echo of "It's possible," reverberating through my body is what struck me with awe. (Hearing him say, "I love you," is great too.)

Forever, my life has been changed by these two words and the little boy who said them. What if we replaced all of the "It's not possible," in our lives with' "It's possible." How would your life change if you were able to remove doubt or skepticism and replace it with belief and dreams?

Most adults come to accept the majority of what happens in life with a solemn seriousness that prevents questioning except for the occasional, "Why me?" Kids on the other hand, usually have hundreds of questions. "Why? Why not? What if? Really?" top the list. Very little comes to them as is, and yet it does. Because they live in the moment of now, acceptance of what is and the possibility of what can be exist simultaneously. Whatever children feel, they feel. If they get a scratch, tears flow amongst screaming and crying that quickly stop with the miraculous application of a band-aid. Then play resumes. If a child gets hurt badly, and has to go to the ER because of a more serious injury like a broken bone, they revel in picking out the color of the cast and getting their friends to sign it. Immediately they question when the cast can be removed and if they can swim or climb a tree while the cast is on. When an adult breaks a bone, often the first thing that comes to mind is what can't be done because of the circumstances, not what can be done.

In fact, it seems that the statements, "It's impossible," and "It can't be done," automatically prime the universe and the child with the reply, "Says who?" and "Why not?" This is quickly followed by, "It can be done, it is possible, and watch me do it." Imagine a world, in which adults retained that sense of wonder and awareness of the infinite possibilities. Problems would be seen as opportunities to grow and as the challenges that they are instead of as insurmountable obstacles. These momentary hindrances would be more like the scrape requiring a band-aid, a brief episodes of aggravation, quickly forgotten so that the rest of life can be lived.

For the next week, whenever life poses you a challenge, can you look at it with the eyes of a child, and see the possibilities inherent in the situation? Can you replace doubtfulness with wonder and excitement? This won't make your life emergency room free, but it will make it less painful. One final hint, if a boo-boo does occur, the colorful band-aids with designs on them do actually seem to make things better much faster than the plain ones.

Saying Yes for a Day or a Lifetime

In this society, often we often say yes without thinking about it. Unfortunately, we say yes so often to things that are not important that we don't have the time or energy to say yes to the important things or to the important people in our lives. Recently I realized that I say "Yes" to others very often, and "no, maybe, or later" to my children because I expect that they will accept these answers and love me anyway. Often by doing this, I was disempowering them. I made a conscious decision to say some form of yes to them whenever possible for one day. Although I expected them to ask for more and more as I said yes more often, they actually asked for less and sometimes independently decided that they really did not want what they had thought that they wanted.

I guess that when they hear "No, maybe, later, tomorrow," or any answer other than yes, they continue to ask for things wanting a "Yes" answer. The difficulty of the request honestly does not matter. "Yes," seemed to work miracles. "Let's figure out how you can do that or have that" worked better than "let's think about that later." After they got a positive answer, they felt empowered, and then they occupied themselves much longer than usual. As a result, more of my time was freed up to do things that I wanted to do. I also noticed how good it felt to help them have what they wanted instead of having to defer their dreams til later.

It also seemed to be contagious. Usually when I ask them to help each other, I get lengthy explanations as to why they shouldn't have to or why it is not fair that their brother or sister gets something. After a while of me saying yes or helping them accomplish their desires, they were more likely to help their siblings without fussing or arguing. Again, as a result, more of my time was freed up again. They cooperated much more and looked for opportunities to help me or each other. It seemed bizarre and surreal. In reality though, when an adult wants something, getting a yes moves them along on their journey. Anything else causes them to go back to the drawing board still looking for a yes.

Even though I had previously believed that by saying no, I was teaching them that you can't always have what you want, I was not teaching them that at all. Nor did I really believe that. I do believe that you can have what you want although it may take persistence and effort as well as conscious choice. They had gotten the part about persistence and effort paying off, and thus their repetitive requests for the same things over and over. By saying yes, or let's figure out how to do that, two other things happened. They were satisfied whether they liked the outcome or not. Also, when they realized that they could have what they wanted, and they did not like the choices that they would have to make to have their desire, their desire vanished without me having to spend any energy or time explaining why they couldn't have it or really did not want it. Contrastingly, when they had heard no, the desire continued to grow in their minds. It is like the old saying that what you resist, persists. By removing resistance, their lives and my life became much easier which was quite contrary to what I was concerned might happen.

For the next week, play with saying yes to the really important people in your life. You may find that this makes yes show up in your life more often as well.

Moving Books

Long ago, I was moving some books from one place in the house to another. I asked my son, Cameron, to help. I gave him two books while I stacked as many would fit in my arms. I loaded them so high that I had to use my chin to keep them from falling. After climbing a flight of stairs with them, Cameron watched as I opened the door to carry them up another flight of stairs into the attic area. With innocent eyes and open heart, he peered into my soul, "You know, you don't have to carry all those books by yourself. I can carry some more of them for you." He took another few books into his arms evening out the stacks that we each carried. His comment was so genuinely sweet that I felt as though I could have carried ten times as many books at once with ease because he was so willing to ease my burden. Just knowing that he was available to help me in that way made me feel as though I could carry more.

After we got the books to their new destination, I tucked him into bed and went to do other things. I could not get his comments or actions out of my head. It was not actually that he carried those books. It was his unselfish gift of himself and his time that touched me. Mostly, it was knowing that I was not alone in carrying out my tasks, knowing that I had his love and support as I did my work. Metaphorically, he was telling me that I didn't have to move all the books or do anything else, for that matter, all by myself, and that help is available often in much larger supply than we realize.

What if help from the universe really is available in abundant supply? What if all we really need to do is ask? Why don't we ask for that help more often? It may stem from the desire to be self-reliant. It may be from believing that if we don't do it that it may not get done, or that others can't do it as well as we think that we can. Perhaps it could be that we don't think that others will help, or because we underestimate their capabilities. Sometimes it is because at times we have refused to help others, and then we feel as though we don't have the right to ask for help. Unfortunately, many times we don't feel that we are worthy of asking for help, as though we don't deserve help.

How often in life do we pile things on ourselves that are not necessary? How often do we try to protect others when they don't need it? Why do we ask so much of ourselves at times when others are available to help? Why don't we ask for more from others?

For the next week, consider what you would like assistance with from the universe. Make a list of things that feel overwhelming or that you don't want to do by yourself. Do you know anyone who would help you? You don't know whether they will help unless you ask them. The worst that they can do is say no, and then you simply ask someone else. If you don't know anyone who could help with your needs, state them to God or the universe. Often this simple act will bring you more assistance than you could have imagined. Remember to offer assistance as well, as it is impossible to give away something unless you already possess it.

Sardine Sandwich

One night, long ago, one of my children wanted to eat sardines. Luckily, I saw him tugging at the sharp lid while standing next to my bed on the carpeted floor. I sent him to the kitchen where his dad safely removed the lid. He got a plate and proceeded to mash the sardines as I watched. I offered him vinegar and crackers, which is how I eat them. He said that he didn't want those. Instead, he wanted bread to make a sardine sandwich. "Okay, he might eat that," I thought. As I saw the gears turning in his head, he stated that he needed peanut butter, cheese, and ketchup to top the sandwich. To finish his masterpiece, he added the delicacy, Cocoa Crispies cereal. As I watched, I knew that he would not eat this concoction, and yet I let him do it. After he took a bite, he twisted up his face and said, "I don't like that. It's horrible." He threw it away, and then he ate a plain peanut butter sandwich.

This child has made many bizarre concoctions, many of which I have been coerced into eating. Once he made a soup out of water, ketchup, and other bizarre and since forgotten ingredients which he seasoned with almost thirty spices. It smelled bad and tasted worse. As I took the first bite, he watched for my reaction, and asked how it tasted. I paused, trying not to vomit, and searched for the words to express my opinion. Thank God, he answered it for me as he took a sip of the soup, and said, "That's disgusting." What I had struggled to say, he said quite elegantly and without hesitation.

Quite often in life we spend time and energy creating something. Even if it turns out differently than we expect, it may still be useful like these articles which often turn out completely different than I have anticipated. Sometimes though, just like the aforementioned food items, our creations are disasters that cannot possibly be salvaged. In our attempt to avoid the truth of the situation, we continue to forge ahead into it continuously convincing ourselves that it is better than we think. Then we spend even more precious time and resources on something hopeless, instead of cutting our losses. (If you have a hard time imagining a situation that can't be remedied, just think of what you could add to that sandwich or the soup that would possibly make them edible.)

Do you have situations in your life that you have meticulously created that just are not what you had dreamed of? Are you forcing yourself to tolerate miserable situations because you can't bear to part with what you have spent so much time and energy creating? If so, is it worth it? Do you have the guts to say and do what my child did, even when I didn't, for fear of hurting him?

For the next week, consider what creations you are living with that you really don't like. Do you have the strength to toss them away? Or, will you stick with them even if they are horrible? Can you even tell the useful creations from the useless ones anymore? If not, consider how you would feel if destiny or fate removed the questionable circumstances from your life without any effort on your part. If you feel relief at the thought of it being gone, it is probably time for you to let it go or discard it. If you can rid yourself of what is not useful, then you have the time to devote to new creations. Otherwise, you will keep spending your valuable life on things that don't serve you.

Cleaning Closets

Long ago, I told my children that we needed to go through their clothes in order to get rid of the things that they had outgrown and make room for new things. With one child, I had to sit and repetitively redirect their attention to the task at hand as we went through each and every item. It took hours. With another child, items were quickly designated to the keep or pitch pile. My third child did not require my help at all. I had expected varying children to need varying levels of assistance; however, I was mistaken about how much assistance each child would need.

In general, each of my children needed a certain amount of help with certain things because of their own level of independence. In this case independence was not the only quality necessary. The ability to let go of the past as well as to live in the present moment was also required. The two children that took longer to go through their clothes relived some of their memories as we went through them. My child who went through their clothes quickly and alone lives so fully present in each moment that they had no need to relive their memories or second-guess their decision to keep something or throw it out.

As much as I would like to say that I was able to quickly go through their things, some of their things were difficult for me to let go of. In life, as well, things may be difficult to get rid of even when we have outgrown them. As I held some of their favorite clothes that they could no longer fit into, tears welled up in my eyes as fond memories flooded into my mind and heart. Even though these things are mere articles of clothing, they are symbolic of so much more. It is the ability of these things to evoke these memories that pull at our heartstrings. It is this that fads and trends are made of. It is this that memorabilia dealers take advantage of as they hope to sell us a piece of a dream or, at the least, something that evokes a sentimental memory.

As I reflected on this process of going through stuff and letting go, I realized that the more fully present that each moment is lived the easier it is to let it go. Also, the more fully that one lives life, the less attachment there is to things. In addition, when something is no longer useful to you, someone else may have need for it; I have found many treasures through the years at yard sales and Goodwill Stores after others had no need for the items. Just as it is easier to let go when you have little attachment to things, it also seems that that those perfect treasures just pop up into your life when there is little attachment.

For the next week look in your closets and drawers. Are there things that are no longer useful? Are you attached to the stuff in your life because they are physical reminders of things that you need to release? If so release them. If they are so very important to your heart, keep them with joy and love. Are there things that you need to purchase? Do you need some memorabilia to remind you of a happier time? Even though the physical item cannot bring back the actual circumstances, it can act as a portal to the memories, and sometimes that is what we need. Whether this is a time for things to come or go in your life, be gentle with yourself and with others, as our things and lives constantly cross each other's paths.

Flushed Away

Years ago, I took my little girl, Alexa into a public restroom. She was terrified to sit on the toilet. I cleaned it off, and she still did not want to sit. I asked her what she was afraid of. She replied that she didn't want to get flushed. Somewhat puzzled, I asked her to explain what she meant. She told me that the toilets without handles (automatic flushing toilets) flushed while she was sitting on them and that she was afraid that she would go down the toilet like the paper. I reassured her that even if it flushed while she was sitting on it, that she would not be flushed away. She was not convinced, so I offered to hold her hand while she was sitting on it so that I could pull her off of it should the need arise. Well, almost immediately after she sat on the toilet, it automatically flushed. She jumped off the toilet and decided that she would wait til we got home to go the bathroom. No amount of pleading or reassurance would budge her wall of resistance. Knowing that she needed to go, we cut the trip short so that she could get to a manually flushed toilet.

Obviously she had experienced this several times previously to be so sure that it would happen again. Even though I routinely carried her to public restrooms, I was oblivious to her discomfort. And as I had never experienced this, I had no frame of reference other than knowing that she would not actually be flushed away. Therefore, I minimized her experience. As fate would have it, I soon got the opportunity to sit on an electronically controlled automatically flushing toilet. As soon as I sat down, this loud noise occurred, the toilet started vibrating, and the water forcefully drained out. Out of surprise, I jumped up and realized why she had been so frightened. Even though I knew intellectually that I was safe, the sudden surprise flushing momentarily scared me.

The point of this story is that we often times dismiss other peoples' fears or concerns because we have not shared their experiences emotionally and because our past experiences have created filters different from theirs. Even when we are physically present as I have been when she has used public toilets in the past, I did not realize how she was feeling even though I vaguely recalled her mentioning not liking the automatic toilets. The reason that I did not understand it was two-fold. First, it was not particularly important to me at the time. Allowing her to empty her bladder was important. Second, I analyzed why she felt this way. After determining that her fear was illogical, I dismissed it. Well, now that it has happened to me, I truly understand why this experience is extremely frightening to a seven-year-old child.

As is often the case, why something has occurred is not always as important as the fact that it has occurred, and that it needs to be dealt with. Understanding others is important, and sometimes impossible. Because our genetic heritage, our brain wiring, and our life experiences are so varied, it is amazing that we can understand each other at all.

For the next week, pay attention when you catch yourself saying, "I understand," and consider the possibility that you really don't understand. When others say it to you, realize that sometimes it is next to impossible to truly understand ourselves, much less understand others.

Hidden Treasures

Years ago, my children went to an Easter egg hunt. My mom and my aunt, Bernice, had an accurate count of the eggs that they hid. The children searched high and low for those eggs, finding them buried in piles of leaves, stuffed in bushes, and perched in trees among other places. Some were easy to spot, while others took more time and effort. After the hunt, the children went inside where their eggs were counted. At least twenty eggs were left. So the kids went back with even more fervor and found about fifteen more eggs that had not been apparent the first time. Even after all these eggs were totaled, we knew that some were still out there. Hungry, and tired of hunting, the hunting ceased, and we ate with candy being the first course.

I remember the same thing happening when I was a child. We searched and searched to find every last egg, yet some could not be found, even though they had just been hidden a short time earlier. Every now and then one would be found months later. Even though the candy was inedible by then, the joy of finding the hidden treasure was undeniable.

Life is like that. We search for things...lost keys, misplaced items, the perfect gift, and life's meaning. Sometimes finding them is easy. Sometimes we must take a short break to take inventory of what we have found so that we know what is still out there when we resume the hunt. After long searches, out of frustration, exhaustion, or ambivalence, we stop searching believing that continuing to search is a waste of more time.

Interestingly, there are things to be gained in the process of searching as well as in the process of ceasing to search. When I speak of searching, I mean how the children behaved the first go round of the hunt. They knew that many eggs were hidden and that they had a good chance of finding some. It really did not matter what the egg contained as long as they found it. As long as they remained aware, success was inevitable.

On the second go round, the children knew that a large number of eggs remained. Each child wanted to find what had previously escaped them. Their senses were more alert than before, and they were more excited when they found an egg this time than they had been earlier when it was easier. However, after that, the excitement had faded, and each child had a bucket full of candy. Even though a few eggs remained, no one wanted to spend much effort looking for those last hidden treasures. The children were happy about their bounty and celebrated it, instead of getting caught up in what they had not found. They were content with searching as well as ceasing to search as their awareness turned from searching for candy to savoring each bite of it.

In life, often we start out like those children, fresh with an attitude that life's bounty is just sitting there, waiting for us. All we have to do is show up with awareness and it will be ours. Over time, we learn patience and improve our skills as we rack up life's trophies each one seeming sweeter than the last. Sometimes like the children at the egg hunt, we grow tired, or the effort becomes too much. When awareness is misplaced, we may even become bitter or ambivalent about searching or overlook the treasures that we do find. Just like those children, if we can retain awareness while searching, as well as when we cease to search, then all that we have can be celebrated. And sometimes, like that Easter egg that is found in the fall, we find what we are looking for only after the search has ceased.

For the next week, pay attention as you search for things, physical or otherwise. Do you have a heightened sense of awareness or are you distracted during the hunt? What emotions accompany you in the search? Do you celebrate when you find what you were searching for? If you don't celebrate, how would your life change if you did?

Beautiful Birth

One evening I was staying late after work to do paperwork. I called home to check on my children and our pregnant cat. One of my boys answered the phone telling me that the cat was probably going to have her kittens soon, saying, "She's meowing loudly, and there's stuff coming out of her butt." As I told him that I would not be home for a while, he hollered, "Oh my God. Something's coming out. She's having the kittens. Something hit the floor. I have to go." With that he was gone. Though I had much left to do, my inner voice told me to go home. Not knowing whether I would make it in time, I left my desk as it was and drove home. By the time I had gotten there, Meow, the mama cat, had had two kittens. Over the next hour or so, she had two more. My kids and I lay on the floor with her as she had the last two. At times she made such a fuss that my children asked me to help her. She didn't need any help; she did just fine birthing those kittens all by herself.

After each one was born, she opened their sac and licked each kitten in turn to clean them off, leaving the placenta intact. In between births, she purred as loudly as I have ever heard her purr. After she had birthed the last kitten, she ate the placentas which my children viewed with amazement, awe, and a pinch of "Ooohhh, gross," and "Why does she do that?" pitched in. As I did my best to explain that eating the placentas helped her to replace her iron stores, they asked more and more questions. I answered the ones that I could, and chalked the rest up to natural instinct and Mother Nature, which seemed to satisfy them. Mama Meow glowed as her kittens nursed. My kids glowed as they watched. One of my sons smiled, hugged me and said, "I can't believe that you came home to watch with us. Thank you."

Though I had planned on working into the night, I realized that I wanted to share this experience this with my children. Too often, I miss things with them that can't be replaced. As I left the office with a sigh, knowing that I would walk in the next morning feeling overwhelmed, I questioned my decision. As we all cuddled in the floor in the afterglow, I thanked God that I hadn't missed this, and received the answer that I had made the correct choice. The paperwork would still be there tomorrow. The birth of those kittens would not wait. Though I have already forgotten which charts I left on my desk waiting for signatures that night, an everlasting loving memory was forged in my heart as my children and I watched those kittens enter our world through the miracle of birth.

Though the miracle of birth occurs daily, we often overlook it. Sure, I am talking about the birth of children and animals, and I am also talking about the fact that each day is like a birth in some way. It is an opportunity to start afresh. With each breath we experience a mini-birth in that life-giving process. What if we could experience that miracle every day, in each breath that we take? What if we look around for the magic in each moment, the new things entering our lives, and our bursts of creativity? Though they may not initially seem that similar, they are all connections to the same universal energy that permeates live births.

For the next week, connect to the mini-births in your life as you breathe new life into each breath. Are you more mindful of other things? By simply paying more attention, you may notice the creation of things even more miraculous than newborn kittens.

Scheduling Nothing to Do

Have you ever seen children playing with boundless energy and wished that you could have some of it? What if you could? Part of the reason that children have so much energy is that they spend their time living in the present moment. If such a thing as a schedule exists for a toddler, no one has let them in on it. Adults explain schedules and the need to be ready at a certain time to toddlers who promptly dismiss the notion and go right on playing wherever they are with whatever is available. Watch preschool children live. They are fully present to each moment. They laugh with passion. They cry with passion. Whatever presents itself to them is used to play in truly creative ways. As children age, more and more structure and responsibility is introduced while the wild abandon with which they live dwindles as does their energy. This is no coincidence.

Just like a child, when you wake up each day, you have a world of possibilities open to you. Children, toddlers in particular, don't care about schedules. They want to eat when they are hungry and sleep only when they are so exhausted that they can play no longer. Contrast that with adults whose lives almost always have a prearranged schedule like going to work or planned events such as their children's sporting or school events. Even when children have scheduled events, they continue to live in the present moment which causes frustration for their parents as the children don't understand why they have to get ready to go "NOW."

In this fast-paced world, we rarely have days with no prior commitments or obligations. All too often even our "free time" has been scheduled down to the minute. Merely reading or reciting the detailed schedule of your life is tiring. When you fail to accomplish everything that you planned to do, you may experience a sense of guilt or failure. These schedules and lists which we have created to help us manage our lives have turned into monsters that devour our lives and souls with have to dos and need to dos.

30

We are caught in between our obligations and our heartfelt desires. Contrast this with children who live as they play, freely and usually without schedules of when to play with which toy. If a toy is in front of them they play with it until they decide to play with something else knowing that they can always go back to first toy. Would your life be different if you chose to play with whatever presents itself?

What would happen if you could occasionally get a taste of living like a child without a schedule? They only thing that you are allowed to schedule is the time off. Setting these days up to clean your garage or get caught up on other things is still planning, so go back to the drawing board. Let your imagination run wild with the possibilities for a few minutes. Then let go of the possibilities without planning to do any of them. Therein lies the magic. When the time arrives, you may choose to catch up on cleaning the garage or lounge around in your pajamas all day. You can do whatever your heart, mind, and soul move you to do during this time. It is your time. The only rule for how to spend this time is that you cannot preplan any of it. Actually planning or scheduling anything breaks the rules. The entire purpose of this time is to reconnect with your soul without any have to dos. This truly "free time" is infused with energy and passion that is often lacking in everyday life. This is energy that we see in children who do not yet have the responsibilities of adult life. Enjoy it.

For the next week, schedule an hour or more per day of "unscheduled" time. Listen to your inner voices when they tell you how to spend that time. Do you notice any change in your creativity or energy levels as you spend that time? Do you notice any shifts in your energy or feelings during your scheduled time?

Down the Hill We Go

When I was a child, one of my friends had a mini-bike. Though that was the dream toy for many children, I remember being so afraid of wrecking it, getting hurt, and having to go to the hospital that I would not drive it. My friend had no fear, and was quite a daredevil on it and in life. She really loved riding that bike and the faster the better. After much begging and pleading, she convinced me to ride it with her after promising "to go slow." Despite the gnawing ball of fear in my belly, I managed to get on that bike believing that we would go slowly. Well, she had this big hill behind her house. Even if she wanted to go slowly down it, I'm not sure that she could have due to the sheer effect of gravity and the steepness of the hill.

As we started down that hill, much to my horror, the bike didn't have slow as a speed. It had fast, faster, and fastest as speeds. The hill seemed to grow into a mountain. The first trip felt like it took forever despite our breakneck speed. When we got to the bottom, I got off. I was still alive, thank God. All my parts were still attached and I had not thrown up though I had thought that I would while standing at the top of the hill. After calming down for a minute, I had a strange realization. Riding down that hill was fun. I liked going fast. In fact, I really liked going fast. (I just didn't want to drive and no matter of convincing would change that.)

After getting past that first mental hurdle, I really had fun zooming down that hill (with her driving of course) and then climbing back up. Many afternoons were spent together riding that motor bike. Eventually we outgrew the mini-bike, and other activities took its place, and yet I will never forget that experience. That was one of my first recollections of having a fear and facing it.

Now I have children. After much begging, one of them got a mini-bike. After even more begging, my son convinced me to drive the thing. That same ball of fear that I had felt as a child welled up in my belly as I reluctantly got on that bike built for a young child.

I managed to make two circles in the yard before almost hitting a tree. Luckily, because I am bigger than the bike, I avoided the tree. I know what it felt like driving that bike, and I can only imagine what it looked like. It must have been hilarious to watch because of how much he laughed at me as I got off of the bike complaining about its poor steering. After it was over, I laughed, and I was elated. I drove the mini-bike, no matter how badly. I actually did it. I also knew that although I enjoyed riding the bike as a child, I did not like driving it, and I would not like driving it even if was the appropriate size.

Though I faced fears in both instances they had different lessons. In the first instance I faced a fear and experienced something that I really enjoyed, something that I would have missed otherwise. The second time, I faced a fear and figured out that I would not have missed anything important to me even if I had not faced it. The point is that you never know the outcome of facing a fear until you do it, and once it has been faced, the fear usually retreats. It is only by doing that which we do not think that we can do that we develop courage and actually find out what we are capable of doing.

For the next week, consider what fears you are staring at. Are there any that you really desire to face? What could you learn by facing that fear? Is the lesson to be learned really what you fear? Maybe you will learn that you are stronger than you think when you embrace fear instead of running from it.

Section Two: Lessons from Others

GROWTH SPRINGS FORTH FROM A BROKEN HEART

Who among us can survive this life without a broken heart?
None who feel, I suppose.

Often when that moment of betrayal or loss rips through us, we wonder whether we can withstand the sudden shearing pain and survive the loss. Sometimes the trauma is apparent while other times its origin remains elusive; nonetheless, we experience heartache that threatens life as we know it. As time passes, we may become overwhelmed by the numbing, aching feelings of separation, separation from others, from Divinity, from ourselves. When this happens, we may become stuck in the injury or its resultant wound.

Whether we are able to stay present with the pain and start the healing process at the moment of injury, or whether we have to explore the primal or other wound, there is the metaphorical spilling of blood. It is the act of breaking, resulting in metaphorical or physical bloodshed that acts as nourishment in an otherwise barren time. Watering the ground from whence we sprang with our tears and bloodshed, new life breaks forth from the wounds of the past life, eventually blooming. Without that loss, the surface may have remained dry and flowerless.

I created this piece during an immensely painful time, remembering to honor the pain without becoming lost in it, knowing that something greater would eventually emerge. As I share this with you, I pray for you peace, healing, and love that knows no bounds.

You Can't Force Open a Rosebud

While out picking flowers one day, I picked a rosebud that was starting to unfold. I gently tugged at the petals to see if I could get it to open a little more. It would not budge. Curious, I researched to see if I could do anything to speed up the blooming process. What I found is that this same question has generated many stories and parables over time.

As I read the results of the research, I began to appreciate the unfolding of life even more. Just like the rosebud, it displays itself in its own time, not when we want it too. Furthermore, any attempt to force the blossom to open early is likely to destroy it. However, with patience, the rosebud will bloom into another equally beautiful creation.

The rosebud is exquisitely beautiful in its own way, just as is a fully opened rose. Both are breathtaking in different ways. The rosebud holds all of the potential of the opened flower within it. The opened flower holds all of the past of the rosebud within it. A fully bloomed rose cannot exist without going through the earlier development of the bud. From the childlike budding state, with adequate soil, water, and sunlight the flower will blossom. Any attempt to force it to do so earlier is likely to cause the petals to fall and the bud to die. Even in its earliest form, the rosebud has everything necessary to create a beautiful flower. This life force and potential is inherent in the seed of the plant that develops into the bud and then into the flower. Once this potential exists, the environment need only support its development.

At times, there are obstacles like weeds that can choke out the root system of the plant. These weeds need to be removed so that the flower can continue its growth. After sources of interference are removed, nature must take its course. Neither force, nor prodding is necessary or useful once obstacles have been removed.

After obstacles have been dealt with, all the flower really needs is natural environmental support to develop. As nature takes its course, the bloom unfolds, and all the petals fall to the earth, decaying to provide sustenance for the next generation. Whether the blossom is without a blemish, or whether its surface is marred from insects gathering a meal, the flower does exactly what it is supposed to do as long as outside interference is not great.

Even when we pick the rose, separating the flower from its roots, it does not prevent the petals from opening. It only changes the location of the beautiful flower. There is a powerful lesson in this. When the flower is left intact and moved, its life continues along the usual path without regard to its location. However, when the internal workings are tampered with, the flower may self-destruct, causing petals to fall early, or it may die if the trauma is great.

If the universal plan is for things to develop at their own pace, then perhaps the best path is removing potential obstacles such as the weeds in a rose garden.

For the next week, consider whether there are obstacles in your life that you can remove in order to allow the natural flowers in your life to blossom? Do you need to cultivate patience, refraining from pushing things or hurrying them along? Are there circumstances in your life that need time and nurturing to evolve? Just as the beauty of a rose blossom is inherent in the rosebud, the beauty of your life is ever present in different forms. Take time to appreciate each of them.

Magical Jewelry Boxes

Have you ever believed that some object held an almost magical quality to it? For me, as a child, it was this black jewelry box with painted scenes on it that belonged to my mom. Dad brought it back from his service in Japan. This jewelry box has many compartments lined with red velvet, and it plays music. The shiny black paint and exotic scenes were like eye candy and captured my imagination even though I had no idea what I was looking at in the paintings. My plain wooden jewelry box paled in comparison.

Each compartment held some of mom's treasure. She had a necklace that reminded me of oyster shells strung together that had matching earrings. There was a necklace that she said was made of aurora borealis because it reflected all the colors of the Northern Lights. Then there was the necklace that looked like a daisy. She had a locket that had pictures of my sister and me in it. There were so many more pieces of treasure. How I loved to look at that jewelry box and into that jewelry box. I would ask mom about the jewelry and where she got it. I seemed much more interested in it than she was, and I never quite understood that. How could she have something so wonderful and not even see it?

Now that I have grown up, when I see her jewelry box it still evokes this sense of awe in me. My own jewelry box from childhood now also evokes a different sense of awe. It also carries its own type of magic that I was unable to see as a child when it was staring me right in the face. My children are much more fascinated with my childhood jewelry box than I ever was then and more-so with my adult jewelry box than I am now. I expect that they look at it quite the same as I looked at my mom's even though it lacks the fancy painting. They want to know about each piece of my jewelry. Where did it come from? Did someone give it to me? Can they have it? It must be the very sparkly and personal nature of jewelry that inspires this curiosity in children. It also must be the desire to develop intimate connections with others, through the sharing of our personal stories.

As a child, I believed that that jewelry box was special, almost magical, because of the way mom treated it. She kept it on her dresser, high up probably to keep us out of it initially. When she looked at it, she got this far away dreamy look in her eyes. I don't even know if she realized that she got that look, and she did. Whenever she opened it and put on some jewelry, I knew that we were going to do something special. Whenever she opened it and went through it with my sister, Jackie, and me, I felt special. Mom probably never knew the magic that she spread when she opened that box. Even now, each time that I put on my own jewelry, I put on some of that magic that she shared with me.

For the next week, reflect on any objects that evoke that magical feeling for you. It may or may not be jewelry boxes. It may be baseball gloves, baseball cards, or old car parts. What positive feelings or associations do they evoke? Can you spread that throughout your own life and share it with others? By bringing that magic and positivity into our everyday life we all have the opportunity to make this planet a better place to be.

Earthquake Cakes

Have you ever had a day that didn't turn out exactly as you had expected? Sometimes great expectations turn into what seems to be a mess. That mess can turn out to be even better than your initial plans, even though it may not feel like that while you are in the process.

While in residency, whenever one of the residents was expecting a child, the other residents would become their surrogate family and host a baby shower for the expecting couple. This time it was my turn to make the cake. The couple's request was for a chocolate cake with cream cheese icing.

The night before the shower, I assembled all of the ingredients and made sure that I had decorations for the cake. I got up with plenty of time to make the cake, mixed the batter, and put the cake in the oven. Everything started out as expected. While the cake was cooking, I made the icing. It did not want to thicken. I added more and more confectioner's sugar but to no avail. As the cake was cooling, I made another batch of icing which was also thin.

I put the cake onto the plate to ice it. It was beautiful. Before my eyes, the cake began to crumble and fall apart. What else could go wrong? I was thoroughly flustered. I did not have enough time to make another cake. I couldn't get the type of cake that they wanted at a bakery on such short notice. In my desperation, I remembered that they were from California, and I thought of earthquakes. I would make an earthquake cake with my crumbled cake and runny icing.

My mess started looking better. I broke the cake up a little more and poured the runny icing over it. I tinted some icing pink and blue and made jagged lines to represent the cracks that come with earthquakes. Instead of setting the decorations on the cake in an orderly fashion, I threw them onto the cake. Even though the cake was far from my original vision, I had to admit that it was pretty and very unique.

What started out to be a disaster, turned out to be the hit of the shower. The couple loved the cake and wanted to know where I had come up with the idea as they wanted to use it in the future. I confessed the details behind the cake, and we all had a good laugh and even better cake. In fact, it was one of the best cakes that I have ever made.

That day, I learned that life brings many twists and turns calling for creativity. Instead of panicking when things don't go as expected, consider the possibilities. At first when the cake began to crumble, so did I. I did not want to disappoint my friends, nor did I want them to laugh at me or my cake. In a moment of desperation, I was able to let go of preconceived notions of how things should be and see just how things were. The cake was in shambles and I could either cry or come up with a solution.

For the next week, when life brings you something other than what you had in mind, consider how can you turn that into a solution rather than into another problem. Can you focus awareness on the situation just as it is? Can you let go of your initial expectations? What are possible solutions? How can you put the new ideas into action? As you brainstorm, be gentle with yourself, as making mistakes is part of being human. Your new solution may turn out to be even better than what you initially planned just as my earthquake cake did.

Out of Ashes

Years ago, my at the time seven-year-old daughter, Alexa, asked me why I looked sad. I told her that the co-op, What Dreams May Come, had had a fire, and that many artists' work had been burned up in that fire. Knowing that I had some things in there, she asked if that meant that I would have to "make things all over again." I replied "Yes," and explained that it was not only my stuff that was destroyed, but a lot of other peoples' artwork and possibly even some peoples' dreams. She paused in reflection as she got this very serious look on her face, looked me straight in the eyes, and said, "Is there any way at all that I can help you?" She then added that she could help me paint some new pictures or make new jewelry. Somewhat stunned by her unconditional compassion, I replied, "You just did help me."

In that moment, sadness for our community's loss was transformed into pure hope. This child was able to see past her desire for me to tuck her into bed, which is high on her priority list, and offer kindness, support, and love. Even though I had been hurrying her along getting her ready for bed, she did not let that stop her from reaching out. She blatantly disregarded my requests for her to get into bed, not because she was playing with toys and dilly-dallying, but because she genuinely picked up on my sadness and cared enough to offer help. In my adult mind, I felt sadness. With her childlike innocence, she saw right past the sadness and directly into the hope with clarity and laser-like focus. Because of the brightness of her light, I was able to see the hope with her.

In a world that is wrought with senseless violence and incomprehensible loss, can you retain the ability to see the seeds of joy in the ashes? It's like the old saying goes, "When one door shuts in your life, another door or window opens." Instead of focusing on the door that just got slammed, look at what lies beyond the other doors and windows. When someone is too low to see through the windows, treat them with the kindness that you would show a tiny child. Pick them up, or get them a stool so that they may see the view as well. If the window appears streaked or dirty, offer them a cloth to clean it. Remember what Alexa said, and quote her often, "Is there any way at all that I can help you?"

How would your life change if you focused on solutions instead of problems? Or hope instead of despair? Or love instead of fear? The actual circumstances in your life would be the same, and yet in altering your perspective, the outcomes to the situations are altered. This difference in thought and perspective has the potential to transform ashes into life just as the mythological Phoenix burned, then arose, reborn from its own ashes.

For the next week, pay attention to the metaphorical doors that slam in your life. It may be that God and the universe have an even better plan for you than you could possibly imagine, and that you may not experience that plan unless you are redirected in life. Dig deep and look for the lessons, especially when you don't want to. Accept kindness and help when it is offered. Then pick yourself up, and look for newly opened doors and windows. Can you help others when doors slam shut in their lives? By looking for the open doors instead of staring at the ones that are shut, and by helping open doors for others, step-by-step, we will make the world a better place.

Watching Dominos Fall

If you are patient in one moment of anger,
you will escape a hundred days of sorrow.
-Chinese Proverb

Life is full of ups and downs. There are moments of great joy and moments of great sorrow. Unfortunately, many of us do not come together as often in moments of joy as is moments of sorrow. It is almost as if tragic events shatter the illusions of separation, so that we may act as a united whole. When events like those shown on the nightly news occur, there is no explanation that offers solace. Questions of why, and how, and accusations of blame are thrown about. Understanding will not come from our limited human perspective, and yet in these moments strangers reach out to each other. Prayers for people we don't know abound. Society pulls together to make the best sense it can out of a terrible situation.

When I initially wrote this piece, our state had just experienced the Virginia Tech massacre. It is hard to believe that it has been over ten years since that occurrence. One tragic seemingly localized event had such a widespread effect. This was seen in the statements of foreign diplomats, as well as in viewing the worldwide locations of the victims' hometowns. Ten years later, vigils and events to remember still occur. One isolated event affects the whole because in reality that isolation does not exist. The threads of human life branch out like the threads in a spider web showing us that all are interrelated. From this one devastating event, the far-reaching implications are easy to see. What if all events, both positive and negative, have this effect on the world as a whole and on all those living in it?

Have you ever seen a child line dominoes into intricate layouts, then tip the first domino and watch all of them fall? Even though the first domino only touches one or two other dominos, the effect

44

is perpetuated throughout the entire series of dominos. Though they fall in a brief amount of time, much more time and effort was spent laying out the dominos. Life events and peoples' behaviors affect others in this same way. What takes a lifetime to create can change in a moment. Keep watching the child after all of the dominos fall, and you see that they start all over again, lining up domino after domino. In life, it is not nearly as easy to put the pieces back together as it is to line up the dominos over and over, yet the process is the same. You start where you are, and do one thing at the time.

If we each participate in our lives consciously, being patient in our anger, we truly will avoid much sorrow. If we lash out every time that we are hurt, we will spread that affliction throughout the population only to come back to us. In times of pain and sorrow, it is very difficult to hold things together, much less to consciously choose our words and behavior. Yet that is exactly what is necessary. In times of joy, and in times of pain, you still have a choice of how to behave with what life has brought to you. Will you spread love, kindness, and support or will you spread fear, hatred, and dissent? Regardless of whether you want this choice and responsibility, it is yours. It always has been and always will be.

For the next week, be conscious about your words and behaviors. Watch for the repercussions of your choices in your life. See the effect of your life on others, realizing that just like the domino effect, much of the impact of your life is far reaching and often out of your own view.

Quilting with Threads of Love

Several years ago, a family friend made quilts for my three children. As we looked at each stitch that had been placed with love, I thought about why handmade quilts are so special. For centuries, quilts were made typically as gifts for special events. The fabric scraps were not specially picked out from fabric stores, but were salvaged from previously worn or used fabric. Quite often the fabric had already lived several lives. Flour sacks were turned into curtains, dishcloths, or articles of clothing. And if fabric was actually purchased outright, it usually wasn't to make a quilt, but some other necessity. Only after it had outlasted its usefulness in these capacities did the fabric make its way into a quilt. And when the quilt was worn and torn, the leftover pieces were turned into pillows or wall hangings.

Each quilt told a story. Fabric swatches brought along their history as they evoked memories of past times. Perhaps the quilt had swatches of fabric from the recipient's parents' and siblings' clothes as well as their own. Sometimes special patterns were used to represent a life event. Other times squares were pieced to tell a story of the person's life by sewing pictures of special moments in the recipient's life. After the squares had been pieced, the quilt was hand stitched with love. Most often groups of women gathered together to quilt the handmade creations. As the quilt kept your body warm, it kept your heart warm as well with a tactile connection to your past. With a keen eye, you may even have been able to decipher exactly who had stitched each area of your quilt.

Now-a-days, most quilts are made in large factories. The fabric has no particular story to tell other than it was woven in a place just as impersonal. Though it may be beautiful to look at, it lacks the soul that handmade quilts, especially those from hand me down fabric, have. It still keeps your body warm, and it's just not the same. Over time, I have been gifted several handmade quilts and have purchased several other old homemade quilts. Though new blankets or quilts may keep me just as warm, I love to look at the old quilts and imagine the clothes that the fabric came from and the people who wore them. As I wrap up in the quilts, it is as though I am wrapping up in a blanket of love whether I know who made the quilt or not.

What would happen if everything that we did in life were infused with as much awareness and love as hand-sewn stitches? Remember that these stitches are not haphazard. They are precise and follow a pattern requiring much time and patience. Even though many individuals work together creating one quilt, the stitches are done in a uniform manner so that the quilt will be both beautiful and functional.

Each of our lives is pieced together like the swatches of fabric used in these quilts. Sometimes we feel worn thin and ragged while other times we feel strong and durable. Some parts are rough and tough, while some are gentle and full of softness. Some swatches are festive while others are dark. All the pieces combined make up us and our lives. And as your life is bound together with all others, will love or fear be the thread that quilts your life?

For the next week, pay attention to the tapestry of your life. How would your life change if you lived your life as these quilts were created, with awareness and love? Would your presence make others feel as though they are being wrapped in a blanket of love? Or would it be like that of the factory-made quilt, functional and yet impersonal with little awareness or love?

Pushing Too Hard

Have you ever experienced pushing a door to open it only to be met with resistance? After pushing it a couple more times with similar results, you realize that it is either really stuck, locked, or that it opens with pulling instead of pushing. If it stuck, it simply takes more force to open it. If it is locked, a key is required to open it. If it opens when it is pulled instead of pushing, further attempts to push it open may result in personal injury or damage to the door. So when a door that you expect to open doesn't open either physically or metaphorically, how is it best to approach it?

Think about it. If you apply excessive pushing force thinking that the door is stuck when it is locked or when it opens with pulling, the door won't budge and you may get hurt. If you use a key to unlock the door when it wasn't locked to begin with, you may actually lock the door, further hampering your ability to open it. Alternatively, if you simply pull on the door when it doesn't open with pushing, most of the time the door will open. This solution is the simplest, takes the least effort, and often brings instant success. If pulling instead of pushing does not open the door, the door may be locked. At this juncture, you must decide if it is purposely locked to keep you out for whatever reason. If so, it may be in your best interest to leave it locked and look for other points of entry. If you know that you must enter, this is the time to use the key. You may already have the key or have to spend time looking for it. If it is locked, simply unlocking it allows entry without force. Again, the solution was simple and easy. If pushing nor pulling, and unlocking the door fails to open it, it is a safe bet that it is stuck or purposely welded shut.

If the door is stuck, it may only take very gentle yet constant force for a short period of time to coax the door to open. Then again, it may require lubricating oil on the hinges to allow the door to swing open. If these methods fail, it may be a sign from the universe that the door has been closed for a long time, and either is not meant to open or that it will require more effort on you part to open it. If this occurs, you have to decide whether it requires the necessary effort to bust it open as that amount of force may hurt you or what is on the other side when it flies open. You may also realize that it is time to call for assistance or tools to get it open. At each step along the way, you must decide whether you are meant to open the door and whether you will continue with your efforts to open it as each step requires more work on your part, and some steps bring the possibility of injury.

Even though the above process is blatantly obvious when there is no closed door in front of you, it may escape you when you encounter the real situation. Think about times that you have seen people keep pushing on a door that says, "Pull." Though the solution is obvious to you, they aren't getting it. Even after discovering that pulling the door will open it, they may still be bound and determined that they will push the door open even when it is not designed to swing that way. Just as the solution to this dilemma is simple, many times the solution to life's problems are as well if we can remember to proceed in a stepwise fashion starting with the simplest and easiest solutions first.

For the next week, pay attention to any "stuck" doors, physical or otherwise, that you come across. Is the "stuckness" part of the problem or part of the solution? Do you need more information or assistance to open the door? Is it a doorway that you are willing to cross? Are you ready for what is on the other side of the door? Is the "stuckness" telling you to look for other options? Follow your heart, whatever it tells you, as you will have to face whatever is on the other side of the door once you open it.

Out of Rhythm

Our lives have become so busy that most of us rely on alarm clocks to wake us each day. For centuries, we had natural cues wake us such as sunbeams entering our windows, roosters crowing, or actually getting enough sleep that our bodies' natural circadian rhythms woke us. We also have arranged our lives so that we eat when it is "mealtime" instead of when we are hungry. Children who are still following their biological clocks don't always want to eat at mealtime; they want to eat when their internal rhythms remind them to eat. Because we are slaves to the clock, we may tell them that it is not time to eat, that we just ate an hour ago, or that we are not a short order cook. Even elimination has been relegated to a time clock. Many jobs require you to use the toilet during your break. School children and teachers have been forced to go in between classes. Our schedules are so packed that there is little down time for spontaneity or doing what strikes our fancy on a particular day.

In our society, we have become so disconnected from our bodies, that there is no wonder that we have tremendous amounts of insomnia, eating disorders, disturbed glucose metabolism, bowel disturbances, and urinary problems among the host of other acute illnesses and chronic diseases. Even though our body is here to serve us in the betterment of humanity, we do not treat it very humanely. We have relegated many of its necessary functions to suit society's schedules in order to conform. This conformity has its price. As the body fights back with symptoms, we schedule an appointment with a health care provider to get help. Many times pills are prescribed because we want to force our bodies into a routine instead of honoring them and getting back in touch with our natural rhythms through lifestyle adjustment.

If you look at the natural order of things, the sun comes up in a cyclical pattern. No amount of begging, pleading, or prodding is going to change when it rises. The moon follows a natural pattern as do the seasons. Even if we want fall to last year-round in a given area we cannot make it so. We can only transport our bodies to different areas in which the natural rhythms are still present albeit different. Even then we have no control over the natural order of things. Non-domesticated animals still honor their rhythms. Many other primitive and non-primitive societies follow their natural biological rhythms. Why do these natural rhythms persist unless they are beneficial? They persist only because they are beneficial and protective to our mental, emotional, physical, and spiritual health.

For the next week, pay attention to your own natural rhythms and signals, even if you choose not to act on them. Determine if you are hungry before you eat and notice when you get hungry before it is "time" to eat. Reconnect with your body's signals that it is time to eliminate, and realize when you are using the toilet out of convenience. What time is it that you naturally get drowsy? Can you go straight to bed then? You may find that if you retire when you naturally get sleepy, that your rest is better and you don't need the alarm clock to wake you. If you do nothing else, realize that our society has gotten so attached to clock time that it has lost sight of the importance of our own biological clocks. Think about what else your lifestyle of convenience could be affecting.

.

Things that Go Bump in the Night

Have you ever noticed how much louder certain noises seem in the usual quiet of the night? One night when I couldn't sleep, I got up to do some things. As I was getting my laptop, the cord struck my desk as I unplugged it. I went to the kitchen to fix a snack, and it seemed as though opening the refrigerator and using the microwave were decibels louder than in the daytime. The door squeaked as I let our puppies out. Everything that I did seemed so loud. Even the noise of my fingertips striking the keyboard of my laptop caused audible thumps.

While these usually unnoticed noises seemed loud in contrast to the nighttime silence, I recalled my first three years in college. My dorm was about one hundred yards from train tracks. As luck would have it, my third-floor room ran parallel to those tracks. Each night at 2:00 a.m. the train roared by, often whistling just outside my window. I woke up every night for the first week. After that, though it passed by nightly, I rarely heard it unless I was up studying.

Why is it that the tap of fingertips on a keyboard seems deafeningly loud at night? It's because the relative competing background noise, or lack thereof, changes our perception of sounds. In times of relative silence, there is little competition, so any noise seems loud. Even though noises do not magically get louder at night, it sure does sound like they do when you are attempting to be quiet and avoid waking others. In the silence, even a pin dropping is noisy. In the hustle and bustle of the daytime, with all of the competing sounds, noises have to reach the level of a dull roar to be noticed.

As humans, our brains have evolved to adapt to ever-changing environments. During my years in college, my brain learned to drown out extraordinarily loud noises. After going through residency and having children, my brain again adapted to the new need. I needed to hear the beeper go off in the dead of the night while working in the hospital with very ill patients. I need to hear my children when they call out for me.

How can it be that a beeper or a baby's cry can wake someone who slept through a train's loud roar? It is not the qualities of the actual sound but what our brains do with them. In college, my priority was learning, which required adequate sleep. I learned how to block out anything that interfered with my sleep. Years later, even though sleep was still important during residency and early childrearing, hearing the beeper or my children was more important, so my brain made sure that I heard them.

We do the same thing in life. We overlook or minimize things that we deem less important while we maximize and focus on things that we believe are important. Over time, a thing's relative importance can change as did the relative importance of my sleep in the examples given above.

For the next week, pay attention to what you notice during the noisy part of the day and then again in the stillness of night. Are you paying attention to the people and things in your life with the highest relative importance or the lowest? Do you need some quiet time for yourself to reconnect with the silence which makes all else sound louder? Or do you need to learn to drown out some of the competing noises when they are not important? As you pay attention to the sounds all around, remember to pay the most attention to that little voice of inner knowing that resides in each of us.

Connecting Separation

Many of you have heard of the mystic Sufi poet, Jalāl ad-Dīn Rūmī, and for many this will be the first time. His poetry is haunting, soulful, and speaks to the many mysteries of life. Much of his writing marries the sacred with the profane and shows the connections inherent in perceived separation. Perhaps that is what draws me to his writing.

In one of his poems, "The Guest House," Rumi encourages us to welcome each new experience into our lives and our hearts without judgment. He explains that even if we believe the experience to be painful or full of sorrow, it may be wiping our house clean for something much more spectacular than what we can possibly imagine. In addition, he reminds us that these experiences come as guides from the universe. In this day and time, or in any other for that matter, we can all benefit from universal guidance. Unfortunately, all too often when that guidance comes disguised or in garb other than what we expect, we judge it harshly, reject it, or cast it out. Instead, if we are able to welcome all experiences with open arms as Rumi suggests, we may gain priceless wisdom and invaluable knowledge.

As I read his poetry, I am reminded of those connect the dot pictures that I did as a child. Initially the page had a few squiggly lines and many dots. Over time, a picture takes shape as more and more dots are connected. It may or may not turn out to be what it initially appears to portray. (If three-dimensional connect the dot puzzles existed, his poetry would actually resemble these much more than a two-dimensional puzzle.) Rumi's poetry does something very similar. It connects the mundane to the spiritual and vice versa mirroring the ebb and flow of energy in the universe between things that initially appear static and yet are bursting with life force. Then, quite often, he brings it right back down to ground zero again.

For a moment, consider a single humble grain of rice and a single bean. Although a single grain of rice and a single bean would hardly constitute a mouthful if eaten in a meal, they could produce large crops over time if they were planted and nurtured in the correct environments with the bounty of their harvest being further utilized to plant more crop areas over a period of time. Tremendous amounts of food could be produced from what initially would not sustain one person. Whether the bean and the rice was cooked or planted, initially they had the same life force.

At some point, their life path changed. Some grains of rice and some beans are cooked and eaten. Others are reinvested to create more rice and bean fields. Both paths are honorable and necessary. Other rice makes its way into wedding party favors, cereal, face powder, and hundreds of other products, just like other beans do. And do you know what? There has been absolutely no fighting or arguments about which rice or which beans got planted or which got cooked or even about which ones got eaten. They have lived peaceably and in our service. What if we all lived peaceably and in each other's service?

Life has many inexplicable connections, like how Rumi, rice, and beans really are connected. Maybe, I'll explore that another time. For now, suffice it to say that when combined, rice and beans have excellent nutritional value and are a meal suitable for any guests that show up on your doorstep.

For the next week, look for connections especially between things that don't seem to have any. Can you find ways to live peaceably and in service to others, especially when it requires stretching your usual patterns of behavior? While savoring grains of lovingkindness in your own life, will you choose to invest a few of those grains to create fields of it for all sentient beings to enjoy?

Shifting Forces

Recently, I had a conversation with a friend. We were discussing how life expresses itself metaphorically. Quite often, what happens externally is mirroring what is going on internally. She related the beautiful example of holding a handful of sand in different ways. If you relax your hand and scoop up sand, you can hold quite a bit of sand. However, if you take that same handful of sand and tightly close your hand, the sand starts leaking out. The tighter that you hold onto the sand, the more granules escape. Even though it would seem that holding on tightly would secure the sand, the opposite occurs.

This got me to thinking about the properties of different things and how they respond to changing forces. Consider holding an uncooked egg. Hold it gently, and the egg retains its shape and contents. Put it under too much pressure, and it will crack. Let it go, and we all know the mess that must be cleaned up. Though similar in shape, a rubber ball will hold its own until extraordinary pressure is applied. If you drop or throw it, it will bounce right back, no worse for the experience.

Sometimes in life, circumstances require a death grip. Other times, merely holding a space is necessary. Some things will shatter when let go, other things will bounce back after the temporary parting. Every object has different properties, just like people. And just like the specific combination of hydrogen and oxygen that forms water, the same substance exhibits different properties depending on the current circumstances and previous experiences. Think of the sand. When superheated, sand, which is free flowing and sturdy, becomes glass. Though it will now hold a shape much more easily, it easily shatters with a blow. The egg, once cooked, is much less fragile and is almost rubbery in consistency. And if the rubber ball is super cooled and frozen, it becomes like the egg that shatters when dropped.

So, which state is the real state of the sand, egg, or ball? All of them are, because these objects do not exist in a vacuum. The same goes for people. Some people allow you to experience your strengths and others your weaknesses. Don't fool yourself. You do the same for others. Unlike objects, people are lucky enough to be able to change their environments and their responses. Many times, you can influence the effect that you have on others. You can choose loving behavior or you can choose malicious behavior.

Interestingly enough, though the behaviors are very different, they serve similar purposes of minimizing pain. Loving behavior minimizes the pain for all involved. That does not mean that it is not painful, only that the behavior attends to the highest and best outcome for all involved. Malicious behavior, on the other hand, is often done because someone is in pain or is trying to avoid experiencing pain themselves. Because of this, they reflect or divert the pain to another. Then it is up to the receiving person to choose how to respond.

Now back to my favorite example of water. The water changes states over and over again. No matter what the water goes through, steam and ice both revert back to water under average circumstances. All of the other objects mentioned, are drastically altered and do not revert back to their original states. People are not objects and yet they exhibit qualities of each of these objects. They are definitely altered by the experiences and circumstances of life, and yet the very essence of who a person is, love, never changes.

For the next week, consider how you affect others. How does their behavior affect you and your subsequent behavior? Even when it is difficult, will you choose loving behavior? If you do, how is your life and that of others around you affected?

Life Happens

Recently a friend of mine graduated college. She remarked that it had been a long time coming as she had been working for some time in a job she disliked while she went to school. Though she had to overcome many obstacles in order to graduate while working, she did just that. Listening to her speak of her graduation, I could hear the joy in her voice, saying that all of the sacrifices had been worth it. Though the journey had been long and at times difficult, the destination had beckoned to her. Shortly after graduating and arriving at her initial end point, she started looking for a master's degree program to complete.

Life is funny this way. Once we reach the destination that we think is the end all be all for us, it transforms into yet another starting point. And once we reach the next perceived end point, the process endlessly starts over. You see, when you take a vacation, you can pick your destination, pack appropriately, and schedule your itinerary. Usually, the destination, not the journey, is the focal point. In life you can set goals, work toward them, and eventually reach them. The problem is that if your only focal point in life is the destination instead of the journey, you miss the majority of your life, which you can never get back. As the old saying goes, "Life is what happens while you plan."

Furthermore, in life, there are so many uncontrollable variables. On vacation, variables are considered as you prepare for it. You may take clothing for different types of weather and plan alternate activities in case unexpected events occur. In life, we tend to have one picture fixed in our heads of how we want our lives to be. When it veers off of that course, we may become aggravated, disgruntled, or downright miserable which makes us even more unlikely to reach our initial goals. My point is that life happens. We may have an idea of what career we would like to pursue, where we want to live, and who we want to spend our lives with. Things happen from second to second that we cannot anticipate, and our entire lives may change. It is our ability to adjust to the changes in life and to appreciate the many states of beauty and goodness that gives life its richness.

You cannot change yesterday, no matter what. Wishing that you could only prohibits you from taking control of today. You may not get tomorrow, so you must live today. Continue to set goals and take steps to reach them, while focusing on the process of living instead of the outcome. Pay attention to the little things in each moment. As you get in your car, smell the honeysuckles. Listen to the birds. Feel the warmth of the sun or the wetness of the rain on your face. Savor the foods that you eat. Feel the softness of your clothes on your skin. Smell the fragrance of your soap. There are countless opportunities each day in which to participate in your own life.

For the next week, consider your own goals. Where would you like to be in six months, one year, and five years? See them firmly in your mind, and then let go of them. Give your attachment to their outcome up to the universe. As you live each day with these dreams in your heart, leave space for the unexpected, realizing that there is a grand scheme of things that is far greater than we can understand with our limited human perspective. When you realize one of your dreams or goals, celebrate it. When one slips out of your grasp, hold the hope that even something better is yet to come. In short, live today as if that is your only goal.

Rituals

As far as documented time has existed, there have been rites of passage that mark certain milestones. Ceremonies celebrating puberty, marriage, and death occur in some form or another in almost all cultures. So, what exactly defines a rite of passage or ritual? And why are they important?

Interestingly, the roots of rite and arithmetic are the same and refer to numbers. Whereas most celebrations are merely parties, actual rites of passages are celebrations with a symbolic meaning occurring at specific intervals or marking a life changing event such as the beginning or ending of something or the attainment of a certain age. In addition, rituals are symbolic ceremonies performed with certain predetermined numerical associations whose meanings may or may not be known to the participants. Using the association of timing, we speak of the daily rituals of eating and bathing. There are rituals associated with gardening such as planting and harvesting with the moon. Rituals are so common that we often forget the symbolic meaning of them. Do you recognize these common rituals and their symbolic significance: tucking your children in at night, saying "God bless you," after someone sneezes, or shaking hands as a sign of greeting?

Rituals have brought order and rhythm into daily life and imbibed it both with a sense of mystery and familiarity. They have been used within the religious, political, and fraternal arenas. Sociologically, common rituals have brought societies together within the framework of shared experiences. Periods of time which could otherwise bring emotional havoc bring stability by means of having recurring celebration. Consider how death rituals provide comfort for the family left behind as well as reassurance of the survival of the departed's spirit. Other rituals are secret and are shared only with a group's members.

Though many rituals permeate our society, we have become so busy that we have forgotten the most important components of a ritual. Again, they occur at predetermined time intervals, mark life changing events, and have a symbolic meaning. Using this formula, here is a ritual that you may choose to incorporate into your day to remind you of your good fortune. As you turn on the water for your daily bath or shower, take a few deep cleansing breaths as you say a prayer of thanks for the soap and water that you are about to use. Realize that many advances in plumbing had to occur for you to have this luxury, and many in our world still do not have running water. Be thankful that you do. As the water trickles and splashes around you, remember the life-giving property of water and the fact that your body is over seventy percent water. Without water, life as we know it would not exist. As you lather each body part, say thank you to this part for its function. As an example, I thank my feet for taking me all the places that I need to go, and I thank my back for holding me up each day. As you rinse off the soap, rinse off your past and remember that today is the only day that you actually ever have to spend. Revel in the life changing possibilities present in each moment of today. It is a day that some do not have. By bringing awareness into our lives, we regain our ability to truly live.

For the next week, pay attention to your own culture's rituals as well as those of other cultures. Are there commonalities? Are there differences? What are the origins of the ritual? Are you willing to experiment with adding simple rituals of gratitude, like the bathing one above? If you do, how does it change the experience of your day?

Pineapple and Ham Pizza

As a child, I hated pizza. Though I liked bread, tomato sauce, and cheese, the combination of these things turned my stomach. Every so often, I would try it again with the same results...I felt sick every time that I ate pizza. My mom was sensitive to this fact and did her best to get me something else when my family would go out to eat. Most times we got something else, and sometimes we got pizza. In fact, one time I remember my mom ordering a bowl of pepperoni for me while everyone else ate pizza. I was expecting the pepperoni like it comes straight out of the package. What I got was almost as bad as the pizza. As the kitchen staff had never gotten an order for a bowl of pepperoni before, they did the best that they could. I got a bowl of greasy cooked pepperoni that I forced down out of pure hunger.

As I got older, I remained hungry at many functions as it seemed as though pizza was everyone else's favorite food. In high school, I finally learned to choke down pizza, though I recalled my childhood memory of that bowl of cooked pepperoni each time that I ate pizza. In college, pizza surrounded me. It is what my suitemates wanted to get when we ordered out. Every club function that I attended with food included pizza. Sometimes, I would opt out of ordering out and cook my meal, and I would eat before club functions. Well one night as luck would have it, I had not gotten to eat supper, and I had a club meeting at about eight o'clock. What do you think that they served? You guessed it...pizza.

This time something changed. One of my friends from California had ordered the pizzas. There was a pineapple and ham pizza mixed in with all of the usual kinds. I was intrigued, as I had never heard of putting pineapple and ham on a pizza. I thought, "I like ham, and I love pineapple." And for some reason, this one was not overloaded with cheese. You could still see the pineapple and ham.

My friend pleaded, "Try it. You said you were hungry." With a skeptical look in my eyes, and hunger in my belly, I gave in. I was hooked on the first bite. Not only could I choke this pizza down, I actually liked it. I almost loved it.

My life changed with that simple revelation. Not all pizza was the same. I could dislike all other types of pizza in the world and still like that one kind of pizza. Now I could actually enjoy eating with my friends because I knew what to order. Before that night, I would never have dreamed of eating pineapple and ham together on a pizza. After that night, pineapple and ham pizza became one of my favorite foods.

I am still amused that something that had brought me such displeasure now brings pleasure. I know that in reality there is not all that much difference in a cheese pizza and in a pineapple and ham pizza, and for some reason, there is enough difference. I think of all the times that I have enjoyed more because I gave in and tried something that I was already convinced that I was going to dislike.

For the next week, ask yourself if you are missing out in life because you have a list of what you like and what you don't? Is there room in your life for you to try new things even when they are similar to things that you dislike? For the next week, open yourself up to new experiences. You might even find out that you like pineapple and ham pizza too.

Pink Roofs and Lilac Trim

A friend of mine gave me a dollhouse after hearing that I had always wanted one as a child, and yet had never gotten one. I put it aside unpainted, figuring that as life settled down, I would paint the dollhouse and painstakingly decorate it. Well, my children decided that it was perfect to play with as it was, and that is exactly what they did. After two or three days, the porch railings were falling off and several pieces of the dollar store furniture were missing legs. Even though I was a little aggravated with my children because of their roughness, I was also happy that they had had so much fun with it. So, one night I glued it all together again with plans of painting it in two or three days.

The next night, the glue was dry, and the house was ready to be painted. Hearing that I was going to paint, my daughter, Alexa, offered to help. As I was opening the dark green paint that I had planned to use on the roof, she looked at it as if to say, "What are you thinking?" She tilted her head, batted her eyelashes, looked up and said, "Can we paint the roof pink?"

Well, I love color, and I had chosen many colors to use in the house. The house was going to have a pink bedroom and a pink hall. I had not planned on a pink roof. I had planned on a green roof. Even though I wanted my way just as much as she wanted her way, my heart opened, and I had a moment of clarity. That house was going to have a pink roof. She practically knocked me down as she hugged me with delight. Through laughter and dripping paint, we painted. After we painted the pink roof, we consulted on what other colors to use, and jointly decided that the house would be aquamarine and the trim would be lilac. Seeing the fun we were having, Cameron joined in and painted one of the interior rooms a mottled blue and green with splashes of red here and there.

What had started out to be my dream had changed. It became our dream. As I look back, I wonder if it would have been as much fun if I had gotten my way. I doubt it. Sure, they would have helped paint, and yet it would not have been with the same joy and enthusiasm. You see, something magical happens when people co-create. Because everyone's input is considered as the group develops its vision and implements its plan, everyone involved is passionate about the endeavor. People want to contribute. You don't have to nag or plead for help. You only have to get out of the way so that others may add their part.

Quite often in life, we each have our own agendas, visions, and goals. The problem arises when we want others to adopt ours as their own. Because our visions are not their visions, we may get their assistance, but not their passion. We want to convince them that our way is the right way. This implies that their way is not the right way and resistance may develop. That night I had my vision. Thank God that I let it go in order to create a shared vision with my children.

For the next week, ask yourself if there are areas in your life in which co-creation would be more useful than holding on to your singular vision. Would co-creating be useful in common daily situations such as bedtime rituals? Would it be useful in your work environment? If so, play with it. As you co-create your life with those around you, may you also have the joy that comes with pink roofed houses.

Ripples in Water

Have you ever watched the ripples on the surface of the water? These vary from the defined circular pattern of water that radiates from a pebble dropped into still water to massive ocean waves. As multiple waves move through or collide with each other, complex geometric patterns emerge. If no more surface activity occurs, then the water eventually stills itself temporarily. Imagine traveling deeper and deeper into the same ocean from which the waves are created. At this depth, you would see the ocean's life moving about, schools of fish, sharks searching for prey, and corals offering protection for other creatures, while still living themselves. The naturally unique fauna moves as if blown by a delicate breeze despite the fact that there is no air movement aside from the occasional release of a bubble from an ocean inhabitant. For a moment, become aware of the stillness. It is calm and almost motionless. This is the true nature and essence of the ocean, even though the surface is choppy and turbulent at times.

While going about day to day activities, such as getting caught in traffic, working with the public or cooking dinner, there are seemingly hundreds of interruptions, which can make life seem turbulent or even feel as though a tornado is going through our lives. Life is often described as a roller coaster for this very reason. At times things are on a high roll and then out of nowhere, (it seems) the climb up suddenly and jarringly changes, going into a downhill spiral. While this is expected and exhilarating on a roller coaster, it is extremely scary when life takes unexpected turns. People experience their lives as a series of ever changing events that may seem serene at times and turbulent at others. Deep within their inner core is stillness and an essence that is never changing. It is this source that connects to the universal deity or spirit.

Consider how people react to the small seemingly insignificant events in their life. Most of these are taken for granted or blown out of proportion. These are akin to the ripples in the pond or huge splashes. To create a wave, either a devastating event must occur in your life, or all of the little ripples must coalesce to form a massive wave. These waves can be both constructive and destructive.

Are there small ripples in your life that can be peacefully observed? Perhaps you can create a few by metaphorically throwing a pebble into the pond of life. Remember that not all ripples are destructive or destined to run into conflict with another wave. Some are merely meant to be enjoyed. Also, the same ocean waves that can seem catastrophic, can offer hours of enjoyment for surfers. It is all in how you look at the seemingly turbulent water. Perspective alone changes, as the physical events taking place in the water remains constant.

For the next week, in your day to day life, ask yourself how can you learn to ride the ebb and flow, enjoying both the calmness and the turbulence. Remember that each ripple or wave that you create infinitely spreads to affect the waters of life that we all surf or observe. Do you see how your choices and behaviors influence others through the ripple effect? Even more importantly, down deep in each of us is an unchanging stillness that is full of goodness and stability. Know this especially when the surface of the water appears particularly choppy.

Consider Your Choice

While writing this particular piece, I have started it many times. I have saved many half-written pages, as I could not get where I meant to with them. Usually even if I start without knowing exactly where I am going, I have a general idea, and I get there or somewhere close. This time, it is as though I got half way there, and then there were so many different paths that I could take with each one that I got overwhelmed with the choices and could not figure out which way to go. I saved each partially written one thinking that the next one would flow smoothly only to have the same thing happen. After this happened three or four times, I recognized the pattern and this article flowed out of that.

Sometimes in life, our path is very well defined and precise. We go from kindergarten to elementary school, to middle school, and then to high school. After that things become fuzzier. Most of us finish high school. Some of us go on to college or trade school while others get jobs. Then there are choices about whether to marry and have children though not necessarily in that order. Where and with whom will we live? What car will we drive? Each and every day presents us with an endless array of choices. Many times we have only one or two options. Other times, our choices appear like the dessert choices at the K and W Cafeteria appeared to me as a child, endless and very difficult to make.

You see this was a cafeteria, not a buffet, so you could not load up on all the desserts. You had to pick one from a vast array. Some were easy to rule out while many others looked great, and I was only allowed one desert, so I best choose well. Dessert choices were first in line and there was no going back. Oh, the dilemma at times.

If only that was the most difficult decision that faced us as adults. As a child, it seemed to be such a difficult task to choose which sumptuous and usually chocolate treat I was going to get as impatient adults heavily sighed and frowned, and now I look back and smile thinking about it. If choosing desert really was the most difficult decision that I had to make, I would be miserable as I would feel trapped and as though I had no options.

The moral is that there is a place of balance in which a person feels as though there are several positive options and yet not so many options that one feels overwhelmed. This place of balance varies person-to-person and situation-to-situation sort of like a seesaw and is ever-changing which makes it difficult to quantify. That is why I had such a difficult time grasping why I could not finish the other articles. Usually the infinite possibilities of the articles don't bother me. They start somewhere, go somewhere, and end somewhere with a useful story. This time, the vastness of the possibilities became overwhelming even though I usually welcome that. So I had to adjust to my brain's quirk this week.

For the next week, consider the path that you are living. Is it well laid out? Do you know where you are going or have you left it open to the mystery of the universe? Do you really have any control over any of it? Are your options infinite or limited? If they are limited, who is creating the limits? You or someone else? When you become overwhelmed, are you able to be gentle with yourself and adjust? Or do you become mentally abusive with yourself? As you walk, make sure of one thing: that it is your path on which you are walking.

Always Remember, Never Say Never

While in my first year of medical school, I watched with disgust as a fourth-year student worked on his cadaver with one hand while eating a sandwich with his other hand. I still remember my sense of unease as I watched this. Silently, I shook my head and said to myself, "I will never do that." Even though I rarely use the word, never, I felt quite comfortable that this was something that I would really never do. As a fourth-year student, I took another course in anatomy as an elective. As the comical universe would have it, while dissecting my cadaver, I gasped as I realized that I had walked into the anatomy lab, put down my Coke, and started working with my right hand as I ate a cookie with my left. Even though I was petrified by what I had done, I laughed so hard that I had to stop eating to keep from getting choked.

Life is full of amusing twists and turns. Usually it is just the thing that we say that we will never do that we do. What we say will never happen to us usually does. And when we "always" do something, we don't do it the one time that it really matters.

Maybe this is the universe saying, "Don't think that you can predict the future," or "I have plans that you don't know about." All I know is that these never and always moments are usually transformative. They often cause us to step outside of our comfort zone and deal with issues that we never believed that we could handle or that we would have to experience. Many times they offer us an opportunity to learn compassion or humility by going through something that we had planned to be spared. The disease that we would never get is just the one that we develop. Our well thought out plans lack room for what we would "never" have to deal with, and yet it shows up on our doorstep anyway.

Sometimes, these things happen and cause us to laugh at ourselves, just like I did in the anatomy lab. Other times, our lives are dramatically altered, like the family who loses a loved one because of murder. What I have come to realize is that there are no guarantees or warranties in life. There is no return policy. What you get is what you get. Now what you do with it is completely up to you. When you find yourself in one of these situations, consider what it is that made you feel as though you would never be involved in it. Usually, there is a place for healing and an opportunity to develop empathy by becoming what you did not believe yourself to be or by doing what you did not believe that you would ever do. And when you don't do something that you "always" do, you can learn forgiveness and tolerance of imperfection as we are all human and all make mistakes.

For the next week, consider the things that you always and never do. At first glance, consider what it is that you are trying to avoid or prove. Now, like you are peeling an onion, go deeper into the real issues. Are you trying to avoid embarrassment, guilt, or rejection? Could it be that you are trying to control things that are out of your control? Are you trying to prove that you are better than someone else because deep down you don't feel good about yourself? Out of these experiences, you may realize that sometimes you learn who you really are by being someone that you aren't. From this place, you may learn to love that which you fear by becoming it and learning true compassion and forgiveness.

Sentimental Treasures

Have you ever seen the movie "A Christmas Story?" In this movie, the father character had been awarded an unusual lamp shaped like a woman's leg. Though this man adored his lamp, his family was not quite so enthralled. Through a series of events, the lamp was broken. Devastated, this man lovingly glued the pieces back together much to the dismay of his wife. Though the lamp had little financial value, and had been broken, it was still of great value to him. It mattered little that no one else liked the lamp or believed that it was valuable. It was priceless to him because he had attached an emotional value to it.

How is it that the same item can be invaluable to one person and resemble something dragged out of the trash heap to most others? It is because of sentimental value, which is the valuing of something because of the emotion or feeling that it triggers. Because emotions and feelings are so personal and specific, the value of these items is impossible to define or predict. This is why so many people are willing to pay a small fortune for certain memorabilia that reminds them of their childhood or other happy times. It is not actually the item that is of such great value; it is the positive feelings and memories that these items generate.

Do you have any sentimental treasures? Things that trigger an emotional response? These may be things that have been passed down for generations in your family or a pressed four-leaf clover that you found on a special day. It may be a lock of hair or piece of jewelry given to you by someone that you love. Whatever these objects may be, they possess tremendous value no matter what their actual monetary value may be.

What if you could surround yourself in things that recreate happy memories? Would all the memorabilia or stuff in the world make your life more joyful? No. These possessions trigger memories that can make you glow from the inside precisely because they are few and far between. Even if you can perfectly recreate an environment or ambience that you recollect with your mind's eye, without the emotional connection, the stuff means very little. When these items trigger an emotional response, they act as a portal between a joyful period in your past and the present moment, which is what brings the positive vibrations into your being.

What if you could live each moment so fully that each and every possession, including your thoughts, which have the power to create form, is at the same time priceless and insignificant? Within this paradox is a secret...all that we have is meaningful, and the stuff itself really has very little inherent meaning. By living this paradox, possessions may enhance your life even though they do not define it.

For the next week, treat the seemingly insignificant items in your life as if they have great value. For example, really pay attention to the toothpaste that you use. Consider all the people involved in creating it, and how it improves your life. Think about how your life would change without it. Now focus on something that you usually consider to be tremendously valuable. If it were suddenly gone, how would your life be any different? Would you really be any different without it? No. The reason is that the physical form of this life is temporary. What is temporary holds no real value. The essence of you, your soul and spirit, is the only thing of real and true value because it is your connection to the infinite and the eternal.

Quirks

Have you ever had to deal with other people's quirks in life? Some quirks are innocent enough like wanting the toilet paper to come over the top of the roll instead of underneath. Even these quirks can turn into a major issue when two or more people battle over different quirks. Consider a family in which one person wants the toilet paper to come over the top and another wants it to come out at the bottom. Unless an agreement or compromise can be reached, even this can turn into a battle. Wonder what previous generations argued about when they had outhouses and corn cobs?

There are enough things in life to get seriously concerned about instead of getting so flustered by funny little habits or preferences. People are starving and living on the street in our great country, and we argue about silly little things. Think about how many disagreements occur over things that really don't matter. Sometimes the issue is to be right or in control. Most often they represent a need to be heard and to have one's opinion be counted and respected. In general, the other person only really wants to be validated and reassured that they matter and that their feelings are respected especially when they are different.

For example, years ago one of my children started painting his fingernails black, much to the dismay of some of my family members who saw it as a need for attention. He saw this on an older child, liked it, and decided that he wanted to incorporate it into his personal style. It is his preference. As odd as my tastes can be at times, I can certainly understand liking things that the general public may giggle at or dislike. Though my parents have probably felt as though I picked out things to personally annoy them, I never decided to like these things in order to annoy or aggravate them. I wore and still do wear what makes me happy. In particular, I remember answering the door for one of my dad's colleagues as a teenager. I had on one of my favorite outfits, a bright yellow sweater with this baggy jumper made out of fabric that looked like multicolored paint had been splashed on it. To finish it off, I had on several pairs of earrings and multicolored socks. To some, including the person at the door, I may have looked like I had stepped off of another planet. To me in the awkward time of puberty, when insecurity reigns, I felt beautiful and confident in that outfit no matter what other people saw. The man at the door smiled, and made a comment or two about my attire. I replied that even if he didn't like what I was wearing it made him smile, and that the world could use more smiles, so it was a good thing. He nodded at me and smiled again with what appeared to be understanding.

My point is that we all have our strange peculiarities and preferences. Most of us have better things to do than go around purposely aggravating others by how we put toilet paper on the rolls or how we dress. We only want to be seen, heard, and respected for who we are.

For the next week, ask yourself if there are people in your life whose differences have caused a sore spot? Would your life be better if you could realize that they are living their life as best they can just as you are? How would your life change if you could embrace their eccentricities as well as your own? You may find that when you spend less time concentrating on what you find odd about them that you spend more time concentrating on what you love about them.

Section Three: Lessons from Life

I believe that most of us only show half of ourselves to the world whether we realize it or not. Children, who have not yet learned to mask themselves, usually show up in their full glory until they learn what is not accepted by their tribe, their culture. Unknowingly, we package up bits and pieces of ourselves until we come up with an acceptable face to put on, if you will. Depending on the situation or the people involved, we may show different halves, and yet most of us don't actually show or share our entirety, our wholeness, at any given time.

Often the side that we hide from others or from ourselves contains our seeds of greatness, long forgotten. Perhaps we judge them as "bad" or not good enough, so we hide them, only allowing them to peek out from behind the curtain when we cannot contain them. Perhaps these parts of ourselves were not valued by our family of origin, and in order to save face, we hid half. Perhaps we fear of our own power, so we cloak it. Not wanting to draw attention or offend others, we hide our shining light. Perhaps we fear being fully known or seen, imagining the pain of rejection if "they only knew me;" so we only share half, imagining that that will prevent self-destruction when we inevitably experience said rejection. What if the rejection that we really fear is not from another, but internal, so we even hide from ourselves? Conscious or unconscious, purposeful or not, most of us refrain from expressing our wholeness.

On the other hand, the half face presents an opportunity. Containing the mystery of the infinite potential, of all that is, you can see or imagine whatever you want or choose. By leaving half unexpressed, your creative force is harkened. Sporting a neutral expression (or not, depending on your own perceptions,) allows for interpretation of the figure's emotional state which seems to change depending on your own internal dialogue and sea of emotion. Perhaps there is a hint of wonder and mischief in her eyes, beckoning you, drawing you in to look a bit longer, questioning which half of you is shared. And maybe, just maybe, she is asking if you are willing to be vulnerable, show up fully, and share more.

The Windows of the Soul

In the course of a normal day, I suddenly became aware that I was looking out of a window. As I looked out, I noticed the window-frame and the screen while I appreciated the view. From this awareness, I was struck by the similarities between what I saw out of the window and what each of us sees from our own unique vantage point. It struck me that when I had heard the expression that the eyes are the windows of the soul, previously I had understood this to mean that when we are looking directly into someone's eyes we are able to glimpse a portion of that person's divinity or soul. Suddenly, I realized that our eyes are also the windows from which our souls' view the world.

My hectic day seemed to slow down as I reflected on this. Through that window, I saw trees and blue sky. I saw grass and birds as well as decorative elements in the landscape. Though the view from that window was breathtaking, I realized that it is also extremely limited. The window-frame establishes the boundaries of what can be seen. Although I can alter what I see out of that window by changing the angle from which I look, no matter how many times I adjust my angle of vision I can still only see an extremely limited portion of our world. Also, even though I don't usually notice the effect that the screen has on what I see out of that window, in reality it clouds my perception of what lies beyond it.

As I thought about this, I realized that if I had never been outside of my house, my experience of the world would be very different. Because I have been outside, I can appreciate the natural elements from my limited human perspective as I look out of a window. Because I have been outside of the boundaries of what can be seen from that window, I know that many things exist that cannot be seen out of it. Because I have removed the screen from that window and looked out of it, I realize that the screen dulls the clarity of what actually exists.

In life, our experiences and our abilities to move about in the world create the boundaries of what we are able to see and experience. As a baby, we are limited in our experiences. As children, the more that we explore and change our vantage point, the more we realize exists. As we move past known boundaries, we see new things and establish new boundaries. As we grow and mature, we realize that what we see in life is limited, though what actually exists is limitless. Over time, if we are willing, we may even notice the screens through which we view the world. Only then do we have the choice to remove the screens and see things more clearly as they truly exist.

For the next week, consider your unique vantage point, your frames of reference, and your screens through which you see and experience the world. To start, choose something as your focus. Really study it. How you would describe it to someone who has never seen or experienced it? Realize that no matter how good your description is, it is still lacking. For example, I can tell you that dark chocolate is a dark brown solid at room temperature that melts in your mouth into a delicious, smooth, creamy, sweet yet bitter substance. Even if you understand what each of those words mean, you still don't really know what dark chocolate is until you have tasted it. Once you taste it, you may disagree with my description and believe that it tastes terrible. Your description of dark chocolate may be totally different. Which is correct? Both are. Reality exists as it is. As your boundaries expand, realize that they are still boundaries through which you experience the world. Just as the view from my window only shows a glimpse of the world, the view from your eyes also only shows a glimpse.

Twists of Fate

This past weekend, I almost stepped on this huge dead spider being dragged off by some type of winged insect. After my momentary fright was gone, I reflected on the turn of fate experienced here. In general, it is the spider's web that catches the insect. However, in this instance the tables were turned. Who knows if the spider died while out of its web becoming an easy meal for the insect, or if the insect paralyzed the spider with its venom? Either way, it was an unusual site. Life is full of these twists and turns. We each have many roles to play. Sometimes we have easy circumstances, and sometimes they are more challenging. Sometimes we are like the spider that has created a situation and is patiently waiting for its bounty. Other times we are like the insect that has gotten caught in the spider's web and feels trapped. Other times, things get topsy-turvy and we are like the spider being dragged off by an insect.

In life, children take advantage of being topsy-turvy. They hang from trees, do cartwheels, and position their bodies into every imaginable way. Except in extreme circumstances, wherever they are, whomever they are with, and whatever they have is enough. They take whatever circumstances that they have been dealt and find a way to enjoy life in a playful manner. And when they are exhausted, they rest. Adults all too often find a way to complain about each and every situation. It's too hot, or it's too cold. This person did not speak, and that person never stops talking. We don't have something that we want or we have stuff that we don't want. When is life perfect? Some would say, "Never." Some would say when things are exactly as they want them to be. I believe that life is always perfect. It may not turn out as we expect it will or want it to. It may bring more challenges than we think we can face. It is filled with moments of terrible loss, sometimes more than we feel able to bear. However, in the grand scheme of things, we really have no idea of the role that we are to play in life. That is the great and scary thing about life. It is a huge mystery.

Just as the spider creates its web, we create our lives. We set out with certain expectations, goals, and dreams. When we knock down a spider's web, the spider doesn't complain; it rebuilds its web over and over until its life ends. Then it becomes part of the food chain. What if we become like the spider and rebuild or restructure our lives when they deviate from our plans instead of complaining about the situation at hand? How would your life change?

Living in this way will not prevent tragedy or turmoil. It will allow you to focus on what you can do to deal with whatever happens in your life. By focusing on the present moment constructively, you can sort through things. From this place, you can determine whether there is a possibility of patching things up or whether there has been a total loss that will require starting from scratch all over again.

For the next week, search out spiders building their webs and really pay attention to their process. Most of them cast a web allowing the wind to anchor the first thread. If that first silk does not attach, they cast another until it does. They have trust in the benevolence of the universe. Then they each have a specific method for constructing their web. No way is better than another, just different. Our lives are the same, all are equal and all are different. And, we all have to start over from time to time. Sometimes the nets we cast bring back bounty and at other times they come back torn to shreds. It is up to us to decide how we will deal with what life brings. What will you do?

The Best Day of My Life

Years ago, I had the privilege of spending the entire day with my children. At the end of the day I asked them if they had had a good day. Two of them replied, "It's been the best day of my life." At first, I thought that I got this reply because I had taken them shopping to spend some money that they had earned. After thinking about it, I realized that I have gotten the same reply on many other occasions when I have merely jumped on the trampoline with them, played video or board games with them, or painted Alexa's toenails. It is not the actual activity, but how they perceive the attention and love that makes the day special.

What if we lived each day with full attention and intention to make it the best day ever? What would it take for that to occur? What if we really appreciated every act of kindness that we experienced? What if we made an effort to practice only kindness and acceptance all day long? What if we could appreciate the little things in life instead of waiting for some monumental act of kindness? At times, we turn molehills into mountains when they are negative. What if we used the negative molehills in our lives as a place to plant a flower and only turned the positive molehills into mountains?

Would life be any different? Sure it would. There is a common habit that if something positive happens, you tell two or three people, but if something negative happens, you tell at least twelve or thirteen. Do the math. If something good happens five times daily, and we tell two people, we have shared happiness and goodwill ten times. Multiply this times the number of people on the planet and it seems like a big number. However, if we have only one bad thing happen each day, we only tell ten people, and then we multiply that times all the people on the planet, then one bad thing has cancelled out the positive effect of five good things. THINK ABOUT THIS. No wonder that we have war and people at odds with each other all too often. Now, flip it and see what would happen if we shared the good more often and the bad less often. Using the domino effect, the general disposition, feelings of kindness, and brotherly love would exponentially increase if we merely magnified the positives and minimized the negatives.

Interesting thought, isn't it? Initially it seems almost too simple to make a difference. It is simple though it may not always be easy. When we are hurt, our usual first reaction is to lash out because anger is easier to bear than pain. Unfortunately, by lashing out, we create a snowball effect of negativity that may hurt others just like you were hurt. This will rob you and others of energy and spirit because later we often regret what we said or did when we initially felt hurt, angered, or betrayed. Even though we may wish to take these words and actions back we cannot. Neither can the person who hurt you. We have all been both the perpetrator and the victim in such situations. It requires discipline, effort, and intention to stop the cycle. However, by doing so, you address the conflict at the source which is really the only place that it can possibly be healed.

For the next week, consciously choose your words and actions especially when you have been hurt or offended. With an open heart, send loving kindness to the perpetrator and give them the benefit of the doubt. Consciously speak with that person about your feelings after you have had some time to think about what you need to say. Once it is done, let it go. Spend the time that you would usually spend passing on the negative things on the positive things. Soon every day may seem like the best day of your life.

Life at Super-Speed

Do you ever feel like your life is on super-speed and will not slow down? Unfortunately, that seems to be more and more common. Routinely I hear others say that they wish that there was a way to put the world on hold, catch up on the necessary things in their life, and then restart the world. Because there are ever-increasing ways to spend our time and money, we have become like hamsters that forever run on a wheel just because it is there. Instead of realizing that the wheel will stop, we go faster and faster trying to keep up. When we collapse because of exhaustion, we seem surprised. At that time, we realize that sleep and rest are options. Unfortunately, we barely recover before jumping right back on that wheel at an even faster pace in an effort to catch up as we feel like we have gotten further behind.

What are we running from? What are we running toward? Why do we need the frantic pace that many of us have become accustomed to? What are we afraid of happening if we slow down? Is it necessary to jam pack every minute with activity?

As society has modernized, many time saving devices have been created. Sometimes they save time and other times they don't. Theoretically, it is much easier to do laundry than it was in the days of washboards and bluing. Even so, I expect that we spend even more time on laundry than in days past. Years ago, people had two or three changes of clothes that they used for everything. Laundry did not pile up, as it couldn't. Now we have work clothes, church clothes, and clothes for after work. Because we have more clothes, we have to make more money to pay for them, as well as for the closet and house in which we store them. Don't forget the added costs of detergents, fabric softeners, washers, and dryers. So, have we really saved ourselves any time or labor? Maybe, and maybe not.

Without getting bogged down in a lot of really amazing physics, consider what happens to time or to our perception of it during life changing moments. Sometimes, time seems to slow down or even stand still as though it may stretch out forever only to slip away in an instant. Which perception of time is real? Both are. I remember learning the principle that the time that it takes to complete a task is the actual amount of time allotted to do it. In other words, if you have an hour to accomplish something, it will take an hour. If you have a week to accomplish the same task, it will take a week. Perhaps the increased time pressure increases our focus. Perhaps we are happy with less than perfect results when we know that we spent one hour on it instead of forty hours. Perhaps having forty hours to complete something that can be done in one hour increases our perfectionistic tendencies without actually changing the outcome. In fact, we may spend many extra hours of work attempting to perfect something that was perfectly acceptable after the first hour.

For the next week, play with time. Become the master of your time instead of its slave. Consciously choose how you spend your time. Pay attention to your work habits. Do you do certain tasks that take time and yet do not add to the quality of the work? Can you eliminate or modify these? Do you need to let go of a need to control every little detail or to do things perfectly? Simple awareness often eliminates time wasters such as endless busyness and allows you to find the expanse of time present within stillness. From this place, you may even find the place where time stands still.

Caught Up In Inefficiency

Recently I was trying to get a tote bag off of the top shelf of my closet which I can't reach even when I'm on my tip toes. Wanting it quickly, I tried a couple of times to grab it with a clothes' hanger. I could not reach it. Then I looked around for something else longer that could grab the handle of the tote bag. All of a sudden, I started laughing at myself. I could stand there for ten or fifteen minutes trying to grab the handle, or I could go get a stool and easily reach the tote bag. So I put the clothes hanger back where it belonged, got the stool and then the tote bag. As I returned the stool to its rightful place, it dawned on me that I might still be looking for something long enough to grab the handle of the tote bag if I had not realized what I was doing. Pretty silly, huh?

As I laughed at myself, I wondered how often we get caught up in doing things like this. We start out doing something that we think will work and that we believe will take only a second or two. When it doesn't work, we blindly keep on trying the same thing that is not working. We might make minor variations like I did when I started looking for a longer object even when a much better alternative would be to do something totally different like get a stool. This time, I realized that I had gotten stuck in a theoretical shortcut. The truth is that I could have stood in that closet and wasted twenty or thirty minutes looking for progressively lengthier and lengthier objects to grasp the tote bag all the while getting more frustrated that my goal was no closer.

Why is it that we keep trying the same thing over and over even when we seem to get nowhere, and when we know exactly what would work? I am not talking about a problem with an evasive solution that requires a lot of creative brainstorming. I am talking about average daily run of the mill dilemmas. Initially, we think that our so-called shortcuts will save us time, energy, or a few steps. Occasionally they do. I could have gotten lucky and reached that bag with my first attempt, and I didn't. Unfortunately, and more often than I would like to admit, these potential timesavers end up taking more time and energy than the albeit less creative known way would take.

In general, I am open to new creative solutions. One caveat is that the new solution must bring some enhanced value especially when it takes longer. Sometimes, fast and efficient is not what is best, like in slow cooked chili. Unfortunately, in much of everyday life as we know it, efficiency and effectiveness is necessary. If we can retain awareness while we go about our tasks, then we may actualize the potential benefit of saved time and energy whether we take the usual path or a shortcut. By maintaining awareness, if the shortcut fails to produce results within a reasonable amount of time, then we can abort the shortcut and resume a known path with known results when we don't have the luxury of extra time to spend on creative solutions or when we must be efficient and effective.

For the next week, pay attention as you complete tasks. Are tried and true methods most appropriate? Would a shortcut be useful? When you get stuck in what initially promises to be a timesaver, maintain awareness so that you know when to abort or do things another way. Even when you realize that you have gotten caught up in a time-wasting shortcut, do the best that you can to laugh instead of cry about it.

The Role of Chance

Chance favors only the prepared mind.
---Louis Pasteur

Quite often, I hear my children say, "Mommy, it was an accident," when they spill or break something. Even though it may have been an accident, their behavior usually prepared things for that mishap. They sit the glass too close to the edge of the table or on the floor where it can be easily knocked over. Or, they lean back in a chair which then topples over.

The words chance, accident, and cadence all come from the same common Latin root word. Chance refers to opportunity or luck. Often people say that they have no chance, when they have not done the work to create their own chances. Other times people refer to a second chance or opportunity in life. "Accident" describes an event that we wish had not happened and that most likely could have been prevented through a change in behavior. Cadence is the rhythmic motion of a sound or physical action. Putting this together, coordinated movement, along with thought out behavior creates opportunity or chance in life.

For example, it is not by chance that I sit here typing this page. I have wanted to write for a long time. Previously, my writing had been confined to my diary and occasional letters. One day, I decided to pursue my dream of writing, knowing that it would take time, energy, and possibly rejection. Over a period of time, I wrote and rewrote a few sample articles. Then, I contacted a local newspapers' editor with my articles. After a brief time, he contacted me, and he offered me the opportunity to fulfill one of my dreams. As a result, I have improved my computer skills which increases my future opportunities or chances. Realize that this work would not exist if I had not dreamed of it, and then done the work to create this chance for myself.

What type of chances are you creating in your life? Are you creating lack of chance through a poor, "Woe is me," attitude, or are you creating abundant chance by believing that challenges are here to spur you on in life? If you have suffered chaos through an accident, is there a way that you can use this to create an opportunity? Remember the saying, "If life is a bowl of cherries, I got the pits." Well stop complaining, plant the pits, nurture them, and with time and patience, you will have your own orchard. If you don't find a way to use the pits they become only waste. Your life is what it is now. You can choose what to do with it from here on out.

Teach your children that they create their chances. Education improves opportunity. If I had not gone to medical school, then there is no chance that I would be a physician. When an accident or mishap occurs, review it and learn from it so that it is not in vain. Make amends or forgive if necessary. There is no benefit in beating yourself up about it if you caused it. Wishing that it had not happened does not change it. The only way to make an accident useful is to reframe it and learn from it. Most importantly, as the rhythmic movement of the ocean makes waves, the rhythmic movement that you make over time will allow you to make your own waves. You may choose whether these waves are constructive or destructive.

Just as a house cannot be built without a foundation, a life cannot either. Creating opportunities for yourself is the way to harness chance. The more that you are willing to learn new skills, try new things, and get rejected, the more chance will pop up in your life.

For the next week, pay attention to chance occurrences in your life. Are they really accidental or is there an underlying cadence or rhythm to these occurrences? Is synergy involved? Are they moving you towards your soul's path or away from it? Do you need to reconsider your direction?

Far Reaching Effects

I have this beautiful fountain that a friend gave me. It has a cracked glass ball that rotates on a flowing stream of water. Under the ball sits a light that constantly changes colors. As the ball rotates, light dances around the room in an ever-changing feast for the eyes and soul. It is beautiful during the day, but it is even more spectacular at night. When all the other lights are out, the entire room glows from that tiny light. Light mingles with the shadows in an ever-shifting pattern. It reminds me of life, ever changing and always beautiful.

The fountain can be likened to our lives. Just like life, all parts are necessary for the full appreciation of its beauty. Remove anything and the whole changes. If you remove the light, the beautiful patterns cease to exist. Replace the cracked glass ball with a clear glass ball, and the intricate designs disappear. Remove the pump, and no amount of water will make the ball move. Without adequate water, the ball will not spin. Each component of the fountain has its purpose in the grand scheme of things and each component affects the action of the whole.

The actions that you take because of the choices you make affect everyone in the entire world whether you realize it or not. Consider the butterfly effect. Edward Lorenz was calculating weather patterns when through a series of events he discovered that almost imperceptible changes in air current, approximately the amount generated by the flap of a butterfly's wings, in a particular location at a particular time, could be the determining factor between calm weather and a tropical storm hundreds of miles away.

If the movement of a butterfly's wings can cause such a large and long-range effect, what makes you think that your life makes any less impact? When you really see with your heart and not just your eyes or your rational mind, you realize that everyone and everything has a purpose, and that all of our lives change when anyone's life changes. This can be a difficult thing to grasp particularly when we realize that our choices, beliefs, and actions have such far reaching implications.

Have you ever considered the consequences of your simple or mindless actions like which household cleaners or towels you buy? Some cleaners are environmentally friendly and disrupt our ecosystem very little, while others contain chemicals that may be considered nontoxic in small amounts, but that may be toxic in large amounts or break down into more harmful components. Consider the amount of people using any product and continue down the line. These toxins along with others pollute our water supply so much so that we are cautioned about how much tuna is safe to eat. Meanwhile more and more mutated animals are found. If you prefer to think about the towels you buy, realize that one reason that American textile production has decreased is that labor is cheaper in many other countries in part because of child labor. If a child begins full time work at times before the age of ten, when will he or she get an education or get to play? Even though these are not your children, they are someone's. As you realize that these seemingly insignificant choices have an impact around the world, consider the effects of your larger and more thoughtful choices around the world.

For the next week, think about how the choices you make affect the world at large. The butterfly goes about flapping its wings without realizing its effect on our world. You can change your world and our world with mindful attention and action.

Surrendering to the Mystery

Have you ever played with interlocking metal brainteasers? Many types exist from inexpensive dollar store versions to intricate artistic creations. In order to solve any of the different variations, you must separate the linked pieces of the puzzle without prying them apart or bending the metal. Then you must be able to put it back together for later use. One day, while picking up my children's' toys, I found one of these. This was a simply made puzzle consisting of two identical pieces. Each was a simple circular loop curving into a straight portion. The circular loops were intertwined leaving the straight ends to each side. It looked innocent enough. I wanted a break from cleaning so I figured that I would take a couple of minutes, solve the puzzle, and get back to what I was doing.

"How hard can it be?" I thought, feeling confident and energized by the challenge. At first it was fun twisting and turning the pieces. After a few minutes, it began to appear much more difficult as I had tried all of the logical maneuvers to separate these pieces. After about thirty minutes frustration had overcome fun, and I put the puzzle in my pocket temporarily so that I could do other chores. This simple puzzle was not going to get the best of me. Intermittently, throughout the day when I needed a break, or when I remembered that I had not solved the puzzle, I tinkered with it again and again. That night, admitting defeat, I held the puzzle in my hands and studied it. As I admired the coexisting simplicity and complexity of the puzzle, I began to hold it differently. What I had pulled dangled loosely. All of a sudden, out of the clear blue, I solved the puzzle. The rings were separate, and I had done almost nothing. I say that I solved the puzzle, though it seemed as though the puzzle solved itself as I watched. The solution couldn't possibly be that simple. I had spent all day struggling with that puzzle. As I surrendered to its mystery, it surrendered its mystery to me.

As I reflected on what had happened with that puzzle, and within me, several things struck me. New challenges excite us and give us energy. When we get to a certain point and the newness has worn off, we judge the situation. It is not as easy as we had anticipated or it has not turned out as we had expected. Discouragement and frustration replace excitement. In time, steady perseverance may bring completion and its associated exhilaration. Other times, we reach a point in which perseverance transforms into struggle. At this point, expending more energy struggling is futile or damaging. Continuing to persevere or to struggle when it is time to surrender, is mentally, emotionally, physically, and spiritually draining.

Though our society rewards struggling and perseverance, there comes a time that we must let go of our struggles. As we let go of the struggle, and surrender our attachment to a desired outcome, interesting things may happen. Many famous scientists and inventors report that their moments of clarity occur when they surrender their own struggles. As I said, in the moment that I gave up solving the puzzle, the solution came. It did not come piecemeal or in a logical sequence. It simply and completely appeared in that same moment.

For the next week, offer thanks for the rewarding situations in your life as well as for the lessons learned from your struggles. Then ask yourself if there are puzzles in your life that you have struggled with too long. If so, when you are ready, surrender your situations and their outcomes to the mystery of the universe, and allow its mystery to surrender to you.

Enlightened Dust

Have you ever watched particles of dust dance within a sunbeam? If so, you have experienced the ability to see something that is usually looked at with a frown in a positive light. You see, most people do not like dust. However, as a young child, I loved dust at times and disliked it at other times. On occasion, I would find something with a heavy layer of dust and take the opportunity to draw. My favorite pastime with dust was watching the particles serenade each other within a beam of sunlight peering through the window. My eyes were fixed on the specs as they floated hither and thither within the beam soon to disappear. It was almost like watching minute diamonds as the dust refracted the light so well. At times it was like looking into the expansiveness of the heavens as the specs reminded me of the stars dancing in the night sky.

Then there were those times that I disliked dust like when my mom would say, "Dust your room. Dust the den." As a child, I could not understand what made her want to get rid of this spectacular creation. As an adult, I understand better. Light dust does not particularly bother me. Thick dust now brings to mind things unused, rooms unused, and possibly life unused. It isn't the dust that particularly bothers me, rather it is the fact that so many things go unused, especially a life. Then there are those who would say that dust is a sign of a life well lived in which the person does not have time to dust. More power to them, and usually huge layers of dust do not accumulate in these situations, for the currents of air caused by movement keep the dust from settling into thick layers.

How is it that something can be positive when viewed in one way and negative when viewed in another? Which viewpoint is correct? Both and neither. As above, dust can be viewed from either perspective and there is supporting evidence for both sides. Even though dust can be viewed from either a positive or negative light, it really is neither. It is simply dust. It is our judgment of the dust that causes us to believe it to be one way or the other. In reality, it is paradoxically both and neither.

If this is the case with something as simple as dust, think about the more complex things in our world. We label things as good and bad, or positive and negative. These labels are useful in describing something in terms of our current perspective of a specific situation that in reality can change at any time; and along with our change in reality may come a change in perspective.

For the next week, do your best to look at things from multiple perspectives. Start with neutral things such as dust, water, or dirt. For example, water is life giving and life sustaining unless you drown in it, or unless it is flooding your house from a broken pipe. Dirt or soil can produce windfall crops or it can stain your beautiful rug. After you get the hang of it with neutral things, move on to more difficult things, tangible or intangible. For example, the position that you take on an argument makes sense to you. A contrary opinion makes sense to the party that takes the opposing stance. From each side the opposite side appears wrong or flawed, while in reality someone watching from the sidelines who is not involved and has no vested interest in either side is able to see both sides as acceptable. So, in essence every situation or circumstance may be viewed with neutrality if you can extrapolate out that far and are willing to do so.

Too Many Choices

Years ago, when writing a weekly column, many topic possibilities came to mind, each of which I dismissed. Soon after each dismissal, another topic popped up. Even though many ideas swirled through my mind, none captivated my soul or imagination. Initially, I was amused at how many possibilities I had available to write about, and I kept waiting for just the right one to assert itself. An odd thing happened. The more possibilities I had floating in front of me, the less I could figure out what to write. Frustration turned into clarity as I recalled learning of a marketing experiment done with multiple jams and jellies. Two sales places were set up. The first had approximately twenty different types to sample and purchase. The second had about six types. The theory was that by giving consumers more choices, they would buy more. Interestingly, quite the opposite happened. The location with the smaller number of choices markedly outperformed the location with the larger number of choices. After the data was analyzed, the best explanation offered was that too many choices led to confusion and ambivalence about the products, therefore leading to fewer purchases.

The challenge of having all those options for articles reminded me of that jams and jellies experiment. It was different than my usual challenge of coming up with even one topic to write about. I had gotten used to that challenge. I just start typing. Sometimes I start out with complete nonsense that eventually turns into an interesting essay. Sometimes I type out my fantasies, hopes, and dreams as a way of connecting to the muses. That night, my brain felt as though it was being short circuited by an overabundance of ideas just like I imagine that taste buds would be after sampling twenty types of jams and jellies. The harder that I tried to stop the ideas, the faster that they popped out, until a sudden moment of clarity occurred and all other ideas ceased.

Life is much the same way. At times, it seems as though our choices are severely limited and progress is slow. During these times, it can be challenging to remain hopeful and connected to the source of Divine love and creation. Life may feel empty or pointless. At other times, things come so fast that the choices and situations seem overwhelming. Your entire life changes in an instant, and the changes keep coming. During these times it may be tough to stay focused on anything. It may be that when things seem difficult or barren, that we have temporarily disconnected from Spirit and need a reminder to reconnect. When things happen at warp speed, it may be the Divine orchestrating our lives in ways that we could not have imagined or would not have consciously chosen. Maybe the universe needs us to feel the slowdown as a reminder of who is really in control of things. Maybe it needs us overwhelmingly busy and preoccupied at other times so that we will get out of its way.

For the next week, think about your life choices like the jelly experiment. If you feel that you have multiple options that you have to choose from, there are several approaches that make it less overwhelming. First, if you go into the store to buy grape jelly, buy grape jelly. If you go into the store knowing that you need jelly or jam of some type, then any type is fine as long as that choice is governed by the preferences of whoever will be eating it. When you are ready for a change from grape jelly, buy any other type than grape. Last if you don't need or want jelly, don't waste time going down that aisle.

Altering Perceptions

Have you ever injured a part of your body and then felt like you keep hitting it or reinjuring it? It is a strange phenomenon. Previously when that part was in good shape you hardly noticed it. Usually you are not actually reinjuring it; you are only realizing how often you had been hitting or dinging that body part on a regular basis. However, as soon as it hurts, it catches your attention.

Life is like that. All too often we focus on the glitches in life instead of the things that are going right. The little frustrations seem more significant than they really are. The bigger problems seem to grow in front of our eyes. The more that we focus on the problems, the more that they seem to multiply. Problems seem to crowd out the things that bring joy and satisfaction until we feel almost numb to anything but misery.

Interestingly, whatever you focus your attention on seems to enlarge and whatever you ignore seems to shrink. When done unconsciously, we actually worsen the perception of our difficulties. Although most of us focus on things unconsciously, this phenomenon can be used to alter your perception of what is going on in your life by consciously ramping up your attention on the good things and intentionally lessening your attention on the less good. (The reason that I phrase it this way, is that from our limited human perception, we have a very narrow view of what good is, and what seems bad today may actually end up being a blessing tomorrow.) Simply shifting your focus from the problem to possible solutions may allow the solution to show itself much more easily.

What if shifting our focus to the good things caused them to multiply? What if focusing on all of our blessings actually caused us to notice even more abundance and prosperity in our lives? Returning to the original example, what would happen if we actually focused on the body parts that work well each day instead of the ones that don't cooperate with us as well as we would like?

For example, the next time that something hurts, focus on how bad it hurts, how often it hurts, and your frustration that it hurts. Then intentionally judge the pain to be a negative experience. In a very short time, the pain usually increases causing you to notice it even more. After this experience, again consciously chose to focus on the pain. Remember how it felt when this pain was not present, and chose to focus on that experience. Busy yourself with other activities. In a short time, your experience of the pain usually lessens. If you hit or bump the part, the pain experience will return into your consciousness and you can again shift your attention elsewhere. Alternately, you can reframe your experience and find the positive aspect in the pain experience, such as giving you an opportunity to appreciate how you feel when pain is not present. Though the pain is still present, it is usually less bothersome. This same exercise can be used for mental and emotional pain as well as physical pain.

Over time if you repetitively do this exercise, you may notice that you have less frustration and pain. It is not because the external circumstances of your life have changed that dramatically. It is because you have consciously altered your experience of your own situations.

For the next week, pay attention to your perceptions of a particular situation. Are there other ways to look at the same situation? Are you willing to look at it from a different angle? As you consider different ways of looking at the same situation, do you notice any differences in your emotional state or your internal dialogue? Pay attention to any insights that occur as you alter your mindset temporarily.

Failure Turned Inside Out

One night years ago I had started writing, typing a half of a dozen articles, none of which satisfied me. Frustrated, because usually it was much easier than this, it came to me that part of life is in accepting what does not work. At first, I tried to force these ideas into workable articles. As I gave up on one idea after the next, I became more aggravated with each failure. Just as I was about to give up on writing until the morning, it came to me that sometimes we can only get to where we need to be through a string of what may be disguised as failures. If any of these other ideas had panned out, this one may never have materialized.

Often life holds joyful surprises, just waiting for our surrender to the situation as it is. With surrender to what is, it is almost as if Heaven opens up and says, "Finally, you are going to get out of the way." Sometimes this surrender can only come after many disappointments and "failures." I put that word in quotation marks because these failures are actually pieces of the puzzle that we call life. Like a puzzle, the picture becomes clear only after many pieces are picked up and rejected because they do not fit where we put them. Later, these pieces, which were not useful initially, actually finish the puzzle and fit perfectly.

Part of our problem in life is that we pick up a piece that obviously does not fit. We move it around trying to force it into place. Even if we can shove the ill-fitting piece into our puzzle, it is clear that it does not fit or complete the picture as we imagined it would. While putting together a puzzle, we remove the offending piece quickly and continue our search for the correct one. In life, many times we do not want to admit that the piece looked like it would fit, but doesn't. We keep trying to make it fit, blocking the space from what actually belongs there. In addition, because that piece is stuck in a make shift place, it can't be where it is supposed to be either.

Sometimes we lose pieces of a puzzle. Sometimes pieces from different puzzles get mixed together. Life mirrors this as sometimes we lose an opportunity that is irreplaceable. Sometimes our lives get so mixed up in others' that we have difficulty figuring out which pieces are ours and which belong to another. Just as sorting out the puzzle pieces takes time, it takes time to take an inventory of the pieces in our lives.

With time and patience, each piece adds to the whole. Every now and again, a critical piece is placed that allows whole scenes to be completed effortlessly in an area that had previously seemed almost impossible. In moments of synchronicity, our life also falls into place in this way allowing possibilities to become realities. As more and more pieces lock together, the pile of unused pieces becomes smaller increasing the chance of successfully placing each piece.

For the next week, consider whether there a situation in your life that does not fit? Are you trying too hard to make it fit? Do you need to surrender to the fact that something is not working? Do you need to sort through the pieces to ensure that they all belong to your puzzle? Are there pieces that fit in a spot and that need to be repositioned? With patience, persistence, and sometimes what seems like failure, the great mystery of life shows itself in the completion of each person's puzzle of life. As you step back to marvel at your completed masterpiece, may the holes be few, and the whole creation beautiful.

Can Junk Mail Bring Meaning?

As a child, my mom would take my sister, Jackie, and I to get the mail each day. She and I looked forward to that with eager anticipation. Maybe one of us would get a magazine, or a letter. If that didn't happen, then we would argue about whose turn it was to open what mom considered "junk mail." Mom did not appear to be nearly as happy about the mail as we were especially those envelopes that she referred to as bills and junk mail. I used to hope that one day I would get as much mail as she did. Well that is one childhood wish that happened. I understand why she was not as delighted to get those bills as Jackie and I thought that she should be and why the junk mail aggravated her. As my children argued about whose turn it was to get the mail out of the box or open the seemingly never-ending junk mail, I smiled inside.

The same thing happened with email. When I first got email, I checked it with excitement. Now I almost groan as I weed through the junk that my spam filter misses as I look for the significant email. As with everything else, too much of a good thing is too much.

How often are we like that in life? We want something until we get it, and we want lots of it. As soon as we get it, we realize that the joy it brings is short lived just as another desire rears its head. Does the cycle ever really end? Not as long as what we are searching for is in the material world. Each day there is an endless array of stuff from which to choose with even more bells and whistles than the day before. Drawn in by these endless desires, many of us purchase or seek out many more things than we actually need or want in vain, searching for something that will satisfy the internal hunger for more, for completeness. For some the desire is for more money or stuff. For others, it is the desire for more freedom, time, or intimacy.

Think back over times in your life when you really wanted something that you eventually obtained. It may have been something tangible like a car, a house, a puppy, or something intangible like more freedom. How did you think that obtaining this thing would make you feel? Now that you have it, do you actually feel that way?

In reality, it is not obtaining the objects of desire that brings meaning. It is the symbolism that we confer on the stuff or the intangibles that gives them meaning. As a child, playing with junk mail was symbolic of participating in the grown-up world. To me, getting magazines and letters were symbols of being special or important. It was actually the internal feeling that I wanted. I only thought that it was the mail.

For the next week, recall something that you have really wanted, and consider what that desire represents. Imagine that you have fulfilled that empty space within yourself whether or not you have obtained it in your current reality. Remind yourself that whatever you have right now, if it is not enough, it never will be unless you find that place of internal contentment. Once you find that place, life itself is enough, and the stuff is only the icing on the cake.

Blank Pages and Blank Canvases

One of the most intimidating things in life can be the unlimited possibilities that come with a blank piece of paper or canvas. Sometimes the first stroke of paint on a pristine canvas or the first written words can be the hardest. It may be because of a fear of making a commitment, fear of failure, or feeling overwhelmed by the infinite possibilities in front of us. In this way, even a clean slate can be frightening. Sometimes this causes us to stare at the blank page or the life situation for way too long. Unfortunately, the longer that you sit and stare, the harder it is to ever get started as doubt creeps in even more so.

If fear of commitment seems to be the issue, remember that art is not always about making a masterpiece from the start, it is revealing the beauty inherent in everything, even when it may not be apparent. Even if it does not appear as you had hoped, you can always layer on more paint which gives the painting more depth. Then, the beauty is both in the process and in the outcome. If you focus only on the outcome, you may never get started or you may miss so much in the act of painting or in living. Also, remember that not everyone is going to like your art or your life choices. Some will appreciate it, some will dislike it, and you have to live with it or change it.

Fear of failure keeps many wonderful things from manifesting. The reach for perfection can become paralyzing. None of us are perfect in behavior, so stop trying to be. Do your best in important areas and do what is necessary in less important areas. Lighten up and have more fun. If you get bogged down with fear of failure, this leads to stagnation. Just like water needs to circulate and flow to remain fresh, so do we. Try new things. Paint a new life. If you hate it, paint the canvas white again and start all over. This is why many masterpieces have been recovered under layers of other paintings. Some people reused what was available in the form of used canvas, and other people were able to use fresh vision to see what lay beneath the surface. If you allow it to be, letting go of your past and of your attachment to outcome, each day can be a new canvas. If you keep painting the same picture, that is exactly what you will get. If you experiment with new techniques and colors, you get something vastly different. Also remember that there comes a time when no more paint should be added to the canvas, and no more energy expended on a life situation.

Infinite possibility may sound exciting, and yet it is the unknown infinite outcomes coupled with the finite amount of time that we live, that may be overwhelming. It is the "what if" syndrome. What if I make the wrong choice? So what. We all do at some point. It is making the wrong choices that give us experience and allow us to make better choices later. Without mistakes, there would be very little personal growth.

For the next week, imagine that your life is a blank canvas, full of unlimited possibilities that only you can create. If you are still feeling stuck, watch a child paint. They paint as if there is a never-ending supply of paint and paper and with so much passion that each creation is a masterpiece, no matter what it looks like; so is each life if we take time to examine and appreciate it.

Living with Preferences or Not

One time when I started to type, the word processor page came up minimized. I could see the wallpaper behind the screen where I type. Even though the program worked fine this way, it was different than what I had become accustomed to. Immediately I maximized the screen. Once there was something familiar in front of me, I felt more comfortable with it. Isn't it strange how something so small can have an impact on us? It is like that in life; we get used to things being a certain way, and then when they change, it can be difficult to deal with.

In this instance, the difference was minor, and I could have adjusted to the different screen as I have done at other times. However, the effort required to reestablish my comfort zone was minimal and the familiarity was useful to my writing, so I chose to adjust the screen. Now if I had originally gotten used to typing with a smaller screen, I may have the opposite preference. Neither one is any better than the other. They are both functional. It is only my preference to type on a specific screen.

In life, many of our decisions are ruled by our preferences. In most cases, this is a healthy option. However, at times we get so attached to our preferences, that we cannot function when circumstances change or when these options are no longer available. In fact, most of our irritation in life comes not from lack of necessity, but from lack of our ability to always get our preferences. Think about that. Most of us don't get up in the morning with no clothes to wear or no food to eat. The clothes that we want to wear may be dirty, and we may be out of the cereal that we want to eat. When this happens, again we have options. We can adjust to what is available and choose to be satisfied, or we can choose to sulk because we do not get exactly what we want.

This principle has been written about in many forms. Abram Maslow specifically wrote about hierarchies of need. You must satisfy your basic needs for survival and progress upwards towards other needs or desires only after the lower needs have been met. For example, most people don't start wanting fancy cars and houses until they have the basics covered. Once these basic needs are met, we start wanting more and more in all areas, physically, mentally, emotionally, and spiritually. These become our new preferences.

Now there is nothing inherently wrong with wanting more unless attaining it becomes your way of judging your own worth or the worth of others. When possessions or situations must be a certain way for a person to be happy, that is a problem as many things in our lives are not within our control. In addition, some people are content with very basic things in life, while others are not satisfied even when they live in the lap of luxury.

It has been said that desire is the root of all suffering. I am not sure that that is the case. It is not necessarily the desire that is the problem, but the attachment to the desire. If one is attached to the desire, then happiness comes when the desire is attained, and happiness is elusive if the desire is not attained. Contrast this to a desire without attachment. In this case, happiness may be present with or without attainment of the desire.

For the next week, pay attention to your own preferences and to those of others. How are they similar and how are they different? In and of themselves, are they necessary? Back to our preferences. Remember that preferences are preferences only. They are not necessities, nor are they guarantees. Just as you have preferences, so do all others on the planet. As you are able to know your preferences without attachment to them, your life may even include attainment of more of them.

Overlooked Miracles

Early one morning, while all was still quiet, I looked out of a window and saw sixteen turkeys enjoying a meal of insects. It was breathtaking. I watched for a while. As if sensing that they were being watched, they quickly finished eating and followed the lead bird back into the woods. Though I have seen these turkeys before, I have never seen them together like that before. What struck me is that they live with me each day and yet I hardly ever see them. If it is so easy to overlook something that is so awe inspiring merely because they are camouflaged in the woods, I reflected on what else may be overlooked in life.

Consider that about eighty to eighty-five percent of our brain activity is focused on our visual perception of the world. If that much brain power is used in seeing, and we still overlook so many things, think of how much we miss hearing or feeling.

As I reflected on this, I thought about how my children have selective hearing, swearing that they don't hear me at times. These are the same children that can hear a bag of cookies or chips being opened from three times as far away. Sometimes we purposely avoid seeing and hearing what we don't want to. Other times this happens without our realization. Think about what you may be missing. What if you are so distracted that you don't see the person walking along the street as you are driving? You may only miss a friendly wave, or you may accidentally injure them. What if we don't hear it when someone who loves us tells us that? Without acknowledgement, they may feel unimportant, and you may lose the opportunity to tell them that you love them later.

Each day because of distraction or the seeming camouflage of life, we miss out on many things. Sometimes what we miss is not important. At other times, we overlook things that are priceless. Like the turkeys, sometimes what we overlook is hidden for a while only to reappear in a moment of stillness. Other times, it disappears forever. Because we don't know when or where these moments of wonder will show up, it is best to live fully conscious of your environment and the people in it.

Is it possible that you are missing out on important things in your life because of inattention? If so, you can change that. First, remain fully conscious as you move through your day. Focus on what is in front of you and on what deserves your attention. Use your eyes as well as your heart to view the world. Purposefully see all that is around you especially when you feel compelled to look away. Listen as though each spoken word that is uttered has the potential to change your life. Chances are that these words may alter your entire life plan when you expect it least. If you don't hear them or see the opportunities around you, you may miss out on the chance of a lifetime.

 In order to magnify your other senses temporarily and possibly longer, close your eyes and focus on other sensations like the texture and taste of a piece of chocolate melting in your mouth. Usually in the rush of every-day life, we may eat chocolate and not even recall the experience. Pay attention to the textures of your clothing and furniture. Feel the skin of your child as they hug you. Smell their unique smell. Immerse all of your senses in living. By staying present and looking everywhere for the wonders of the universe, you are much more likely to see and experience them.

For the next week, pay attention to your own awareness of your environment and the people in it. Do you see things that you have previously overlooked? Do you hear things that were previously imperceptible? Do you notice feelings, previously unfelt? Are there miracles unfolding around you that you have missed?.

Epilogue: Writing a Life

I have always loved to write. As a child, I remember the feel of my pencil trailing across the lined paper. I still love the smell of pencils being sharpened, and the warmth of an eraser after it has been dragged across paper. With pencil in hand, I longed to write with the permanency of ink. I can still see the flowing blue ink that came from my first Bic ball point pen. Shortly after that glorious day, I got a calligraphy pen and learned how to write as most of our forefathers had written. As I moved through these stages, I learned the ins and outs of each instrument. While it was true that the pen could make more permanent markings, fixing mistakes made with them was more difficult. Correction fluid, better known as White Out, also had its allure until you had had to use it several times. It seemed to take forever to dry and left conspicuous markings almost as noticeable as striking lines through my errors.

Over time, my love affair with pens, pencils, and paper has evolved. Though I still love the feel of fountain pen ink stretching across parchment, I have learned that crayons and markers will also do the trick in a pinch. Moreover, I have found the convenience of a computer.

Though I do not get the same tactile satisfaction from a computer that I get from pen and paper, it has several features that blow these other instruments out of the water, most notably the editing features. Before the computer, my mistakes were always visible after I made them. No matter how gently I erased, or how meticulous I was with the correction fluid, the corrections stood out where errors had been. And if I didn't catch my errors, you better believe that my teachers would catch them and emphasize them with their bright red ink. With my computer's features, I can make huge messes and with the touch of a couple of keys, no one is the wiser. Furthermore, if I don't like the order in which I wrote something, I can rearrange everything in a matter of seconds.

If life was only so easy as to have delete, backspace, and editing features. Initially it sounds great. You goof. You delete. You do it over and no one is the wiser. You wish you had traveled before you had children. Hit edit, and rearrange the order of your life. After you correct and rearrange your life, to an observer, it appears perfect. Unfortunately, you still know the secret. Your behavior has not been and is not perfect. You have made mistakes and your timing has been off. Since no one else can see this, there is all that pressure to maintain the illusion of a life with no mistakes. And since your life appears perfect, no one cuts you any slack.

Compare this with reality. We make mistakes every day. Some are almost invisible. Some are blatantly obvious. There is no back space, delete, or edit. Sometimes we can fix these mistakes easily. Other times, there is no fixing that can be done. We have to draw proverbial lines through them and move on. As painful as it can be to have to see our mistakes and the results that stem from them, it is useful. Because of the visibility of some of our mistakes, it gives us a chance to learn humility and compassion through shared experiences. It offers us the opportunity to teach another so that perhaps they will not have to make the same mistakes.

From now on, as you write the story of your life, be creative and deliberate. Use loving eyes and a loving heart as you reflect on the portions that you wish you could edit out. Even more, celebrate the clear and error free portions.

ABOUT THE AUTHOR

Teresa Moore is a physician, teacher, healer, mother, writer and artist. From an early age, she has labored to integrate western medicine with holistic healing, believing that health encompasses the "wholeness" of body, mind, and energy. With a gift of seeing the world slightly differently than most, she brings a fascinating, funny, touching, and timeless world of wonder to her work.

Teresa has practiced allopathic medicine for over twenty years in rural Virginia while including many holistic approaches in her healing practice. She is level one certified in Reiki and has completed coursework in medical intuition in addition to her medical degree. She has personally practiced aromatherapy and various types of meditation for over thirty years and is fascinated by the mind-emotional-physical-spiritual body connections in health, wellness, and disease.

She has been on the faculty of Edward Via School of Osteopathic Medicine, associated with Virginia Tech, for over 10 years serving as a preceptor for underserved care. Twice she has received the award for Clinical Educator of the year-Southside area, presented by the classes of 2015 and 2016, and has individually precepted over 80 medical, nurse practitioner, and physician assistant students through her position with Virginia Tech and other institutions.

Teresa wrote a philosophical column "Life on Purpose," for The Southside Messenger from 2006-2011, as well as having many articles published in ECHO. In addition, she wrote a healthcare column for Footnotes, a towing and recovery trade magazine for a couple of years.

Having had many experiences for growth in her lifetime, she has used these experiences to help others especially in times of transition. She has presented workshops, seminars, and keynotes at the local, state, and national level focusing on personal empowerment and how our beliefs shape our lives, as well as how to survive the curve balls that life sometimes throws us.

ABOUT THE PUBLISHER

Dedicated to changing our world – one person at a time

Turning Point Healing Retreat Center is an educational facility located in rural southern Virginia. Its mission is to provide a wide range of holistic workshops, classes, and modalities for the physical, mental, and emotional empowerment of all participants. Our programs are for families and individuals impacted by trauma or addictions, those experiencing pain and facing physical challenges, and those who seek a new path for personal growth. The bucolic environment provides a quiet, safe, and nurturing setting that offers a pathway for change, growth, and personal transformation.

For more information visit us at **www.TurningPointHealing.org**

www.ingramcontent.com/pod-product-compliance
Lightning Source LLC
La Vergne TN
LVHW021514080426
835509LV00018B/2516